W9-AMQ-249

P R A Y E R
T R E A S U R E S

Discover the Riches of Prayer

D O R O T H Y   E A T O N   W A T T S

Pacific Press Publishing Association
Boise, Idaho
Oshawa, Ontario, Canada

Edited by Bonnie Tyson-Flyn
Designed by Tim Larson
Cover photo by ©Tony Stone Images/Michael Orton
Typeset in New Century Schoolbook 10/12

Copyright © 1995 by
Pacific Press Publishing Association
Printed in the United States of America
All Rights Reserved

With the exception of quotations from the Bible and the writings of Ellen G. White, the author is responsible for the accuracy of all facts and quotations cited in this book.

Watts, Dorothy Eaton, 1937—
     Prayer treasures : discover the riches of prayer / Dorothy
Eaton Watts.
          p.   cm.
     Includes bibliographical references.
     Spine title: Watts prayer treasures
     ISBN 0-8163-1271-0 (pbk. : alk. paper)
     1. Prayer—Christianity. I. Title. II. Title: Watts prayer
treasures
BV210.2.W35   1995
248.3'2—dc20   95-18289
                                                          CIP

95 96 97 98 99 • 5 4 3 2 1

Contents

Introduction

The Treasures

The kingdom of heaven is like unto a merchant man, seeking goodly pearls (Matthew 13:45).

E very country has its national treasures. Prayer Country is no exception. "Christ has a treasure house full of precious gifts for every soul,"[1] but how often these treasures sit gathering dust, undiscovered, unclaimed!

When Mary, Queen of Scots, fled to England on May 16, 1568, she took with her a valuable string of black pearls given her by a cherished friend.

After Mary was beheaded a few years later, Elizabeth I, queen of England, asked her private agents to find this necklace. They tried in vain to locate it. Since then, hundreds of private investigators, officials of the British Museum, and Scotland Yard searched for the missing national treasure. For 350 years, its whereabouts remained a mystery.

Then one day two young American women, Lavinia and Lucy, of New Haven, Connecticut, were touring England. In the town of Newhaven, they wandered into the dusty secondhand shop of Martin Lazenby.

"Do you have something small and inexpensive that we could take back to America as a gift for a friend?" Lavinia asked.

Looking around the cluttered room, Lazenby noticed a dirty string of beads hanging from a nail in the wall. Taking it down, he offered it to them. "This isn't much, but it is small, and I can let you have it for a shilling."

Lucy bought the beads, thinking they might have possibilities if they were restrung and cleaned up a bit. The next day she took them to a jeweler in London, who promised to have them ready by the next morning.

When the young women returned, they were invited into the manager's office. There, an official of the British Museum told them the story of the lost necklace. He said, "We have found the missing pearls. We will give you twenty-five thousand dollars for them."[2]

Can you imagine how Martin Lazenby felt when this news reached him? For years, those beads had hung on his wall, but he didn't know the value of the treasure he possessed.

The treasures of Prayer Country await those who make unhurried daily tours of this great land of the soul. They remain hidden to the casual visitor. They elude the person who goes only on group tours but are there for the one who visits the King of Prayer Country alone. For such, the King has untold riches of the spiritual life.

The more we visit Prayer Country, the more we realize that there is yet much to discover about the hidden depths and possibilities in prayer. This book will not focus on the material things we so often request, but rather on the precious prayer treasures God has for us, such as peace, joy, acceptance, grace, forgiveness, direction, friendship, patience, and courage.

PART ONE

Exploring
Devotional Prayer

1

Pursuing God

You will seek me and find me when you seek me
with all your heart (Jeremiah 29:13, NIV).

For more than fifty years, I have pursued God. There are
three places where I have found Him. Each place was
different; His role was different; and my purpose for seeking
Him was different too.

Place one
When I was five years old, I knew exactly where God was. He
was in heaven. Heaven was just above our chimney top, just
above the treetops. I visualized heaven as a sort of third story
to our house. Heaven seemed so near that during a thunderstorm I thought God was simply moving His furniture around.

One morning when Mother called me to a breakfast of
oatmeal porridge, I protested, "I don't like oatmeal porridge!"

"Too bad!" she said. "That's all there is."

"Then I want bananas on my porridge." I pouted.

"Sorry. We have no bananas," she replied, pouring milk on
my porridge. "There are no bananas in the store."

"Why?"

"Because there is a war going on. All the ships are busy
taking food to the soldiers across the ocean. There are no ships
to bring bananas for Dorothy."

"Then I'll ask Jesus to send me some," I declared.

Daddy laughed. "Well, young lady, until He sends you some

bananas, you'd better eat your porridge before it gets cold."

I ate my porridge, then ran outside to play. I remember standing under the big maple tree in the front yard, looking up at the heavens and telling God, "Please send me bananas."

The very next morning, Daddy had a surprise for me—bananas! It was the first shipment to reach the stores in many weeks.

Where did I find God? In His heavenly department store. I pictured Him there in His store waiting on customers, finding things I wanted and sending them down to me. He had bananas, dolls, roller skates, and lost kittens in His storehouse. All I needed to do was ask, and He would fill my order.

When I later read that "prayer is the key in the hand of faith to unlock heaven's storehouse,"[1] I felt that I was on the right track. In those days I truly believed that God would supply my every need and wish—all I needed to do was ask.

I held on to this view of God for the next twenty-five years. However, the longer I lived, the more disappointments I experienced. God didn't always fill my orders.

I prayed for a new Sabbath dress and got it the same day. But I prayed for a baby, and I couldn't get pregnant though we tried for many years. God supplied me with a job but seemed unable to supply the miracle of life for a man I had hit in a traffic accident.

In the book *Prayer Country,* I shared my disillusionment with God.[2] Because He no longer filled all my orders, I gave up on prayer. For two years, I stopped pursuing God. When I decided to search for Him again, I discovered Him in a different place, fulfilling a very different role in prayer.

Place two

By now, I had a more sophisticated view of God. He was now millions of light-years away, past billions of galaxies. I found Him on His throne in the center of the universe.

I pictured God as the king of the universe, sitting on His great throne in the sky. Here was a God to be reckoned with! It was important to be on His side, so I did my best to prove my loyalty to Him: I tried to keep His laws. I went Ingathering. I taught a Sabbath School class. I led a youth group and visited the sick. In exchange for my loyalty and untiring service to my Leader, I figured I was due certain advantages. I figured He owed me one now and again. He could pull a few strings for me. So I came "boldly before the throne of grace."

My God was more powerful than any ruler on earth. When we needed to get Canadian passports for our three adopted children without leaving our mission field in India, God worked a miracle.

"It's impossible!" the Canadian officials in New Delhi told my husband. "You'll have to go back and establish your residence in Canada."

"Please write a letter on our behalf," Ron asked.

"We'll do it, but we don't think it will do any good," the official responded.

But my God worked on our behalf. Within three weeks, we had Canadian passports for our children, and we didn't have to leave the country. God did that for us! He was an awesome God of miracles!

At another time, my three children and I were in Jackson, Ohio, at my mother's home. My husband Ron was half a world away in Bangalore, India. A legal matter came up, and I urgently needed to talk with Ron. The problem was that we had no phone in our house in Bangalore. There was a phone at the mission office, but it was Sunday.

I phoned the office anyway, but of course no one answered. Getting on my knees, I cried out to this mighty God of the universe. I pleaded, "Please, God, come through for me. Send a message from Your throne to Ron. Get him on his scooter, and send him to the office. I'll give You twenty minutes to get him there, and then I'll try again. I need to reach him desperately."

While I was still on my knees, the phone rang. It was Ron! He had felt impressed to call me! Absolutely amazing!

For the next twenty years, this is where I found God—on His throne in the center of the universe. What was He doing there? Overseeing the affairs of the universe, operating a giant switchboard of prayer, working things out for me long distance.

What was my purpose in seeking Him? To get miracles, to solve the really difficult problems of life that I couldn't handle on my own.

Place three

May 22, 1987, in my fiftieth year of life, was the night I found God anew. I was sitting alone that Friday night, wishing I could be traveling with my husband. Bored, I walked around our house looking for something to read.

I picked up *Ordering Your Private World* by Gordon MacDonald.[3] At two o'clock the next morning, I put the book down, enthralled with the concept that God wanted to come into my life as a close friend and companion. Gordon MacDonald suggests that a good way to build this relationship with God is to write out prayers and meditations on Scripture in a journal. That Saturday evening, I bought two blank books and started journaling.

The experience of keeping a spiritual journal revolutionized my relationship with God. For the first time, I began having a living, personal relationship with Jesus Christ. Before, two minutes was my limit for prayer; now, I can easily spend two hours.

I had come to place three in my quest of God. Where did I find Him? Right here on earth, wherever I am—in the bedroom, in the car, in the kitchen, on a plane, at my computer. Why do I seek Him now? Just to experience His presence, to know Him better, to love Him more, to share my life with Him.

In place one and place two, I was looking for miracles; but now I am looking for God Himself. For once I have found Him, I have found all that really matters. Of course He still has His storehouse. He still is in control of the universe. But best of all, He is here with me, my Friend and my Companion, through all the joys and trials of life.

A recent experience

On Monday, July 12, 1993, I recorded in my journal that I would visit the doctor for my annual checkup. That morning, I wrote something in my journal that I've never prayed before:

Lord, please, if there is any little problem inside of me that needs fixing, help them to find it.

My mammogram showed a small lump in my right breast. Further tests revealed that it was cancer. Plans for a trip to Europe had to be canceled, and within two weeks I was in the hospital for a lumpectomy. As I wrestled for the first time with a sense of my own mortality, I was sure this was the end—and I even doubted I would see my next birthday.

"Go on to the Ukraine without me," I told Ron. "I know I'm going to die, but I'll surely last three weeks until you return."

Bless his heart, Ron didn't go. I needed him so much as I struggled with the pain and the emotional upheaval that followed my operation. Something went wrong. Blood vessels leaked, and I became swollen and turned black, blue, red, purple, and green. I felt awful and figured I would die soon.

It was during this time that I turned to a "Palms Down, Palms Up" prayer, one of the most meaningful ways I have found to experience the presence of Christ. (I describe my discovery of this type of prayer in the book *Prayer Country*.)[4]

I wrote out the following prayer in my journal, then read it back to God. The first part I read with my palms down, indicating my desire to drop all these things at the fect of the Saviour. The second part I read with my open palms up, indicating my readiness to receive from Him the blessings He was ready to give.

Palms Down: Here's my worry and anxiety, Lord. I don't know what's going to happen about my treatment. They have scheduled me for radiation. You can have all the worry, Lord. It isn't helping at all!

And You can have my body, especially my right breast. It is painful, purple, and ugly looking. Inside is cancer. Lord, please, accept this awfulness, this enemy to life!

I'm also concerned about my speaking appointments and writing deadlines. Lord, You have called me to speak at two women's retreats this fall, and I don't see how I can do it. What can I do but lay the whole problem at Your feet? Here it is, Lord. Take my concern.

Palms Up: Now, Lord, I need to receive from You a sense of Your presence, lifting the load, working things out.

I need Your healing. Please touch my poor, sore, struggling body with Your touch of life. Give me Your love and life right down into my poor, twisted, deformed cells.

I need Your wisdom for myself and my doctor. Help him to know what is the best treatment. Help me to know how to cope with my responsibilities.

Since then, God has worked marvelously for me. When the time came for my scheduled radiation treatments, the cancer clinic phoned to inform me they thought I was clear of cancer and no longer in need of treatment. Instead, I was told to have regular mammograms every six months. To date, all has been clear. Praise the Lord! I feel better than I have felt in many years! God is so good!

One of the most meaningful ways God showed His power in my situation happened in the same week that I wrote my Palms Down, Palms Up prayer.

I was still feeling sorry for myself. But at Ron's urging I rode along to the Fraser River to watch the sunset while he walked our golden retriever Matt along the dike.

It was a sunset of such overwhelming beauty that I began to cry. The peace of the scene contrasted starkly with my tumultuous feelings. My tears flowed freely, and my throat ached. Focused on my pain, I forgot that God was still in control. I forgot that the discovery of my cancer had come in answer to prayer: a lump so small that it could not be felt could easily have been missed.

As I watched the gold change to softer shades of apricot and mauve, I thought of Ron and Matt walking off into the sunset of life without me. How would Ron manage? Poor, poor man!

Then a new thought struck me! He wouldn't manage! He'd find another woman. The thought brought on a new torrent of tears. I pictured another woman walking through *my* house, sleeping in *my* bed, setting the table with *my* dishes, sorting through *my* closets, and spending the money *I* had saved. *I'll have a shopping spree and spend every penny before I die!* I decided.

Just then, I heard the rapid beat of feet on the hard path. Through my tears, I could see Matt racing straight toward the car. When I opened the door, he lay his head on my knee and looked up at me with those wonderful, adoring eyes as if to say, "Whatever is wrong with you, Dorothy?"

I forgot my self-pity as I tried to get Matt to go back to Ron. But he refused to leave me. Amazing! He was always the one out in front of the pack, leading the way. Somehow Matt sensed something was wrong, and he wanted to be there for me.

I felt warmly cherished. In that moment I seemed to hear a voice speaking softly to my fearful heart, "Dorothy, I'm here too. I will never leave you nor forsake you. I am your forever Friend!"

Explore for yourself

1. Think back over your own life's quest for God. Do you see any similarities between your experience and that of the author of this book? When have you related to God as a Storekeeper? A President or King? A Friend? Have you found God in other places and related to Him in ways not mentioned? Try to divide your life into stages of your pursuit of God. Think about how your relationship has matured.

2. Try to think of a hymn or chorus that expresses your relationship with God at different times in your life. Songs such as "He's Able," "Lead On, O King Eternal," "O Let Me Walk With Thee My God," and "O Love That Will Not Let Me Go" each speak of a different reason for seeking God.

3. Read a biography of William Miller. At one point, he pictured God as an absentee landlord. Discover how Miller learned that God wants to become involved in our lives, to answer prayers.

4. Read *Life Sketches*, pages 20-42, about Ellen Harmon's search for the presence of God.

5. Can you think of Bible characters who tried to find God?

These texts will get you started: Job 23:3; Jeremiah 29:13; Isaiah 6; Malachi 3:1; Matthew 2:2; Mark 16:6; John 20:15; Luke 23:8; John 12:21. What purpose did each person have in finding God? Where was God when each person found Him? What was He doing?

6. Make a study of the psalmist's search for God. The following psalms refer to this pursuit: psalms 22, 24, 27, 40, 42, 70, 83, 105, 119. Copy the verses that express something of your own experience in seeking God.

7. Write out a Palms Down, Palms Up prayer of your own. Read it back to God, palms down as you imagine yourself dropping each worry at Jesus' feet. Then pray with your palms up, signifying your readiness to receive what He has to offer you. Ask for the blessings you need; then wait in silence to see if there is anything else He would like to give you.

Explore in a group

1. Think back to a time when prayer was a simple matter of asking and receiving, as it was in the author's place one. Share a time when God opened His storehouse and sent you something you needed or wanted. Try to remember one of your earliest experiences.

2. When did you begin to wrestle with the silence of God, His seeming unwillingness or inability to give you what you so desperately wanted from Him? How did you resolve this conflict?

3. Have you at some time in your life shared the author's concept of God, the mighty Ruler of the universe for whom no difficult problem was too difficult for Him to handle? Share a time God "pulled some strings" for you.

4. Can you identify with the author's experience of seeking God for the joy of His presence rather than for the miracles He can perform? How did you develop this personal relationship? Share a time God was a real friend to you.

2

Searching for Reality

Thou shalt love the Lord thy God with all thy heart,
and with all thy soul, and with all thy mind
(Matthew 22:37).

I met Tina at a Christian women's retreat. "I don't know what's wrong with me," she sighed. "I've tried praying, but my prayers don't seem to go anywhere. Prayer seems to work for other people, but it doesn't seem real to me. Do you know what I mean?"

"Exactly," I said. "I've been there. I can remember times when my attempts at prayer have seemed like a charade, like the acting out of a script. I didn't feel that I could reach out in prayer and touch the living Lord. Nothing seemed to happen. Was God real? Was He there? Did He care?"

Tina nodded. "But now you make it sound so real," she said. "What happened? What made it real for you?"

"Whole-brain praying," I answered. "I discovered that prayer started to become a living reality for me when I began using both the right and left hemispheres of my brain in seeking God."

I then shared some of the following concepts from the book *Whole-Brain Thinking.*[1] These concepts were reinforced at a seminar conducted by Arlene Taylor.[2] Suddenly I knew why sometimes prayer had seemed so real to me.

Left brain

We know that the left side of our brain controls verbal skills,

17

reading, writing, naming, and ordering. It is the part of our brain that analyzes things and reasons from cause to effect. It keeps track of time and sequence. It defines words. It is our rational, scientific, logical side.

Much of our school experience traditionally has been directed to developing the left side of our brains. Also Sabbath School lessons and sermons usually address the left side of the brain. Studying theology is a left-brain activity. Most sermons lead us step by step to a conclusion, defining, reasoning, trying to make biblical truth logical so that we can make a rational decision to follow it.

The left hemisphere likes rules, theorems, and formulas. Not long ago I was a guest on "Life Quest," a radio talk show in Yakima, Washington. One caller expressed her difficulty in overcoming smoking. She had read that if you prayed St. Jude's Prayer for nine days straight, you would stop smoking.

"Is this the correct prayer?" she wondered. "How important are the nine days? How important are the exact words?"

This is an example of an extremely left-brain view of prayer. The caller was hoping it would be a formula guaranteed to work. But prayer is not a set of words or a sequence of activities. It is not a formula for getting what you want in life. Rather, prayer is a spiritual experience, a relationship with God.

Don't misunderstand. Understanding theology and doctrine is vitally important. However, such knowledge does not get to the very heart of the spiritual experience. A left-brain understanding about God is not what we are searching for in prayer; instead, we are looking for the miracle of a relationship with God Himself.

I believe that our devotional life requires our whole brain to be involved in our search for God. I believe that our prayer experience will become more real as we begin to use the right side of our brains, along with the left side, in our pursuit of God.

Right brain

Research shows that the right side of the brain is involved with symbolic thinking. It is the side that deals with spatial images, music, and artistic images. It is our creative, emotional, and spiritual side. It is the hemisphere that sees likeness between things, that understands metaphors and parables. The right brain is the intuitive part, the part that brings us to a knowing of something without a rational basis for our conclusion. It is the side that makes a sudden leap of insight, that allows us to see the invisible, to accept a miracle.

We balance a checkbook with the left side, while we visualize the face of a friend with the right side. We learn to read the notes of a musical piece with our left brain, but we feel the rhythm and the mood of the music with our right brain. We learn a person's name and facts about him or her with our left hemisphere, but we gain a sense of how that person feels toward us with our right hemisphere.

It takes both sides of our brain to have a complete understanding of our world. I maintain that it also takes both sides of our brain to experience a relationship with God.

With this concept of whole-brain thinking in mind, the command to love God with our whole mind takes on a fuller meaning for me. In Matthew 22:37 and similar references to the "whole heart" or the "whole mind" or "all your heart," I hear the command to love God not only with my rational, scientific, factual left brain, but also with my emotional, intuitive, relational right brain.

Whole-brain prayer

For some, whole-brain praying may mean spending more time in reading and studying Scripture to find the reason for their faith. However, many need to include much more of the right brain in their seeking God, for it is there that we understand relationships and the spiritual experience.

Metaphors and parables

Think of how Jesus opened up the right side of people's brains to His message through metaphors and parables. A fig tree, a coin, a lamp, a sheep, and a mustard seed became visual representations of spiritual truths. Stories of farming, cooking, marriage, and feasting were all used as parables to present a spiritual message.

We can look at any common object and ask the Lord to speak to us a message for the day. For example, I spent over an hour one morning meditating on a stone I picked up from my garden path, along with the passage in 1 Peter 2:5 comparing me to a living stone. As I imagined the journey that pebble might have taken from Creation until it appeared, now worn smooth through the centuries, to make my garden lovely, I wrote the following prayer.

My life is a stone, unpolished at birth, worn smooth by toil and trouble. Lord, how often You have picked me up, a stone in Your hand, and I have resisted.

I have not wanted to change, not wanting to be dropped in a new place, to serve a new purpose, or to feel new polishing elements.

Lord, make me more like this pebble—patient, surrendered, willing to be anything You want me to be. It matters not if I am a stone buried under earth for drainage, a rock among others on a garden path, a thing of beauty in a stone hearth, or a precious gem in a monarch's crown.

Lord, I am willing to be a stone in Your hands. Place me anywhere You desire. Polish me as You see fit. Make me whatever seems good in Your sight!

Music and rhythm

Beverly Moody shared with me a difficult time in her life when she fought against depression and despair. At that time, God led her to do something unusual. She put on some cheerful Christian music and skipped down the hall in time to its rhythm. The upbeat tempo, the cheerful words, and the involvement of her body in skipping were actions that came mainly out of the right side of her brain. Like the lame man healed at the gate beautiful, she rejoiced and leapt before the Lord. In doing this, God somehow seemed more present and real to Beverly. She sensed Him there beside her, lifting her spirits and strengthening her for what lay ahead.

How well I remember my days as a student literature evangelist in southern Ohio. I often walked miles along winding country roads, lugging my heavy briefcase and singing:

> I walked one day along a country road,
> and there a Stranger journeyed, too.
> Bent low beneath the burden of His load—
> It was a cross, a cross I knew.

Jesus seemed very real to me through the power of song. I could sense His presence with me, lifting the load and giving me courage to knock on yet another door. I could hear Him whisper the words to my heart, "Take up your cross, Dorothy, and follow Me to the next house."

Often in times of great sorrow, trouble, or loneliness, I have turned to the words of hymns that were a prayer expressing my thoughts and longings more beautifully than I ever could. Music is one way to use my right brain to worship and to develop a relationship with God.

Art, drawing, painting

Frances Ridley Havergal stood in front of Sternberg's *Behold the Man* in an art gallery in Düsseldorf, Germany, and felt strangely moved. As she looked at the vivid portrayal of Jesus before Pilate, she scribbled out what she sensed Jesus was speaking to her that day:

> I gave My life for thee,
> My precious blood I shed,
> That thou might'st ransomed be,
> And quickened from the dead.

Gazing at the crown of thorns and the blood trickling down Jesus' brow, she wished she might wipe His forehead and comfort Him. She tried to put into words the loneliness she saw in that face.

> My Father's house of light,
> My glory-circled throne,
> I left for earthly night,
> For wanderings sad and lone.
> I left, I left it all for thee,
> Hast thou left aught for Me?

The Saviour seemed very close to her that afternoon. Her heart beat faster as she sensed that He was trying to help her understand the terrible agony He had endured. She wrote:

> I suffered much for thee,
> More than thy tongue can tell,
> Of bitterest agony,
> To rescue thee from hell;
> I've borne, I've borne it all for thee,
> What hast thou borne for Me?[3]

She put the scribbled poetry in her pocket. But when she read it later at home, she felt it wasn't good enough to express the profound encounter she had with God in the art gallery, and she threw it into the fire. Amazingly, the paper drifted out of the fire onto the floor, where her father picked it up and urged her to keep it. The words were later set to music and appear in many hymnals.[4]

I have found that not only can God speak to me through the paintings of accomplished artists, but that I can speak to God in a very real way through my own drawing. Sketching is another way I have found to open up my right brain to love and worship God.

For instance, one day when I was at a crossroads in my career, I felt the need to offer all of my talents and abilities back to God as a gift of consecration. I sketched a gift package onto the page of my journal. Inside that package I put all that I wanted to surrender to God that morning: my spiritual gifts, talents, skills, abilities, education, health, experience, desires, strengths, personality, and creativity. I offered Him my ability to write, organize, teach, speak, and encourage others. Under my sketch I wrote:

I'm all Yours, Lord! Where do You want me to use what You have given to me? Please take away all my concern about this particular appointment, and give me Your peace and assurance of guidance and the certainty of Your leading.

My worship experience that morning was a precious, hallowed time. Looking back, I see that the Lord has chosen to use my gifts of love to Him that morning in a way that I never imagined possible!

Emotional experiences

Sometimes our pain is too deep to form a spoken prayer. At such times, we can simply go to the Lord and cry before Him, just as we would with a beloved friend. Charles Spurgeon calls tears our "liquid prayers." He says, "Open that bursting heart and let it out in tears, if words are beyond thy power."

Commenting on Psalm 147:9, "He giveth . . . to the young ravens which cry," Spurgeon says, "God hears the young ravens; will he not hear you?"[5]

We are counseled to bring our wants, our joys, our sorrows, our cares, and our fears to the Lord.[6] As we begin to share our deep emotions with God, we will find Him becoming very real to us. Sharing our honest feelings (joy, pain, anger, frustration, grief, or whatever) with the Lord is another way we can use our right brains to experience the reality of God's presence.

Explore for yourself

1. The word *heart* in Scripture refers to the thinking, reasoning, feeling part of our body—our brain. Thirty-one references to doing something with "all the heart" are listed in *Young's Concordance.* We are told to love, praise, serve, walk, obey, seek, turn to the Lord, trust, and pray with our whole heart or mind. Look up these ten sample references: Deuteronomy 30:6;

Psalm 9:1; 1 Samuel 12:24; Joel 2:12; 1 Kings 8:23; Psalm 119:69; Proverbs 3:5; Psalm 119:10, 58; 1 Kings 14:8. Use a concordance to find twenty-one more texts.

2. Sit in one room of your home. Look at each object in that area. Ask God to communicate a message to you, using one or more objects as a metaphor for spiritual truth. How does that object remind you of your relationship to God or His relationship to you? Try to find a Bible verse that teaches the same truth.

Experiment for one month, finding a different message from God for each day. Sketch the object; write out your prayer of response.

3. Search for a prayer song that fits your own experience. Use it for a week as part of your personal devotions. Sing or play it. Sing or hum your prayer as you go about the day's duties.

4. Picture word meanings. Choose a word that has several different meanings. Try to sketch its meaning; then jot down a spiritual message God gives you from that use of the word. Try to think of a Bible verse that supports the message. Some words to try are *cross, grace, green, rest, spring, rock, cup.* Here is one example: Light: (1) light bulb, that which dispels darkness; (2) sun, that which gives warmth; (3) weight, that which is not heavy; (4) touch, less pressure.

5. Present God with all of your emotions. Go through a day and think of the various feelings you have experienced. List each one and a brief description of the circumstance. Give each circumstance and each feeling to God. Share your day with Him. Some feelings you might include are frustration, anger, annoyance, concern, anxiety, sorrow, joy, satisfaction, humor, and gratitude.

Explore in a group
1. Think of a time when God was very real to you. Try to remember everything about that encounter with God. Try to identify how your whole brain was involved in that encounter. Make particular note of ways the right brain was activated through music, poetry, metaphor, rhythm, visual beauty, crea-

tivity, intuition, new insights, or emotions. Share your experience and analysis with the group.

2. Provide a brown lunch sack for each person in your group. Inside each bag place a common household object. Have each open his or her sack and spend a few moments in quiet meditation and prayer about that object. What spiritual message can be told with that object? Try to think of a Bible verse that teaches the same lesson. After five minutes or so of personal meditation, have each person share his or her thoughts with the group. Or give each member an empty sack, and allow about ten minutes to find an object and to come up with a spiritual message.

3. Choose a short biblical story. Read through the story in your group. Discuss the story from a right-brained perspective. What sounds do you think you would have heard had you been there? Was there anything you could have tasted or smelled? What emotions were each of the characters feeling? Where do you see yourself?

3

Sensing Reality

I cried with my whole heart; hear me, O Lord
(Psalm 119:145).

Susie had been put to bed, but she'd used the usual tactics to stay up longer. First it was, "I need a drink." Five minutes later it was, "I have to go potty."

Coming to the end of her patience, Mother said, "Susie, that's the last time you get up. You've got to go to sleep."

"Mommy, don't go," Susie pleaded. "I'm afraid."

"Now, honey, there's nothing to be afraid of," Mother assured her. "Remember, Jesus is right here with you, looking after you."

"But, Mommy," Susie whimpered. "I can't see Jesus. I need somebody that's got skin on them. I want someone to hold me and talk to me."

Did Susie express the way you sometimes feel when it comes to prayer? You can't see the Lord, and you so want to make contact with a God who is real. You need to sense Someone there beside you, Someone you can see, hear, and touch.

Job had that experience. "Oh that I knew where I might find him! that I might come even to his seat! I would order my cause before him, and fill my mouth with arguments" (Job 23:3, 4).

Fifteen-year-old Ellen Harmon had a similar experience. For three weeks she had been seeking God, but she could not experience the reality of His presence. Then a dream gave her hope.

She seemed to be sitting with her face in her hands, thinking, *If Jesus were upon earth, I would go to Him, throw myself at His feet, and tell Him all my troubles. He would have mercy on me. Then I would love and serve Him always.* Then a door opened, and an angel spoke to her. "Do you want to see Jesus? Follow me."

In her dream, the angel took her up a steep stairway and through a door into the presence of Jesus. She saw Him smile at her. She felt His touch of compassion. She heard Him say to her, "Fear not." She was overcome with joy as she experienced the reality of Christ's presence.[1]

Learning styles

In our search for reality, we first need to discover how we perceive reality. We know that information enters our brains through our senses: sight, touch, hearing, taste, and smell.

Recent research shows that individuals prefer various styles for learning and communicating: auditory, visual, and kinesthetic. One study showed 40 percent as visual learners; 20 percent as auditory learners; and 40 percent as kinesthetic learners.[2] Another study found 10 percent were auditory, 15 percent were visual, and 75 percent were kinesthetic.[3] Still another study found 30 percent visual, 25 percent auditory, 15 percent kinesthetic, and 30 percent mixed.[4] The percentages vary according to the age, educational level, or culture of those studied.

Communication is more real to us when we are using our preferred sense. The more we make use of all our senses, the better chance we have to get an accurate perception of reality.

Relationships grow best when individuals relate in their preferred communication style. Whole-brain nurturing of relationships, whether on the human or spiritual level, will do much to improve the relationship.[5]

In spite of these differences in learning and communication preferences, schools and churches frequently communicate in a manner that favors the auditory person. That means that visual and kinesthetic individuals must use a less-preferred sense and will have difficulty in finding the experience meaningful.

For years my own devotional life was an up-and-down experience. Sometimes I really felt I made contact with God, but much more often I sensed that I was not connecting properly. I believe now that the times I was closest to God were those when I experienced whole-brain praying, using both hemispheres of my brain and all of my senses: auditory, visual, and kinesthetic.

Although I am highly visual, I am working to develop my auditory and kinesthetic right-brain spirituality as well. Pursuing this goal has been a rewarding experience for me. I believe that as we involve all of our senses in our pursuit of God, we will have a greater sense of the reality of His presence.

Biblical models

With this exciting new concept in my mind, I began searching Scripture for examples of whole-brain prayer, references that included auditory, visual, and kinesthetic methods of praying. My first discovery was Matthew 7:7: "ASK and it will be given to you, SEEK and you will find, KNOCK and the door will be opened to you" (NIV, emphasis supplied).

ASK (auditory)

To ask is to make a request or petition. Asking is basically an auditory activity, involving the mouth and ear, in an attempt to speak to God and have Him hear. This traditional idea of prayer—words we say to God in a verbal, auditory, abstract exchange—is satisfying for approximately 20 percent of the population.

For fun I looked up auditory words in a concordance, words such as *voice, hear, say, speak*. I found forty-one columns of texts referring to auditory communication.

Next, I looked for biblical characters who were auditory. I regard Paul as a left-brained auditory person. He preferred to set out his arguments. He emphasized definitions and reason. David seems to me to be a right-brained auditory person. He loved words, metaphors, poetry, acrostics, and music.

SEEK (visual)

To seek is to find out, search out, look for. Seeking is mainly a visual activity involving the eyes. Visual people want to see God or some visual evidence of His presence in their lives. About 40 percent of people need to experience God in this way.

My concordance search next focused on visual words such as *behold, see, look, appear, vision, eye, and search*. I found forty-nine columns of texts referring to such words.

Daniel, Ezekiel, and John the Revelator used visual means to communicate God's message. They used parables, object lessons, and drawings to communicate truth. God used the wilderness tabernacle to give the children of Israel a visual representation of the gospel.

Sanguine Peter must have been a visual person. Immediately after he denied his Lord, Jesus communicated with him simply through a look. Another time, Jesus used the object lesson of a fish to teach Peter a truth. He also asked Peter to feed His sheep, a visual message. This tells me that God communicates with each of us in the way we will most readily receive it, through our preferred communication style.

KNOCK (kinesthetic)

To knock is to pound on something with the hand, and it involves the sense of touch. It implies hope that there is Someone on the other side of the door. The one who knocks wants to meet God, touch Him, feel Him, experience Him in his heart. About 40 percent of the population need to find God in this way.

In my concordance search, I looked for kinesthetic words such as *feet, hands, heart, tongue, taste, feel, touch, walk, and do*.

I found forty-eight columns of references.

Thomas must have been a kinesthetic person. Remember the experience in the upper room after the resurrection? Thomas claimed that without the opportunity to touch Jesus, he could not believe the other disciples' reports of having seen and heard Jesus.

Three examples

At the British Columbia camp meeting one year, I asked

several people, "When is God real to you? Describe a setting in which you have experienced the reality of God in your life."

Pauline Hunter said, "It's when I sing a song of praise from my heart to God. Usually these times I am alone, simply voicing my love and praise to God. He seems so real to me. My song is a prayer of praise. I talk directly to God, and I sense that He hears me. Then I open His Word for study and hear Him speak to me."

God is real to Pauline through an auditory exchange—singing, talking, listening. She could identify with Psalm 39:12: "Hear my prayer, O Lord, listen to my cry for help, be not deaf to my weeping."

Phylis Stoyanowski told me, "I sense God is most real when I am in nature. I look at a majestic mountain, and my thoughts immediately turn to God. Sometimes when I'm arranging a bouquet of flowers, I look into the heart of a flower, and I can see God and feel His presence."

God is most real to Phylis when she is looking, seeing, and visualizing. She would respond easily to words of Scripture such as, "Look unto me and be ye saved," and, "Thou God seest me."

I am also a visual person. My spiritual journal is full of visual reminders of my relationship with Jesus. Pretty leaves I've collected on a walk show me something of His love. Pressed flowers remind me of quiet times I've spent with Him. I often use sketches to visualize my need. Stars beside requests quickly show me the requests God has answered. Leafing through my journals, I can actually see how God has worked in my life.

Elizabeth Andrews told me, "Sometimes God is so real that I can feel His arm around me, holding me close. Often as I go about my work, God seems so physically present with me that I talk out loud about whatever is on my mind. Recently I felt His presence when He worked a miracle for us in allowing us to stay in our house after the owners sold it to someone else. When God works dramatically for me in this way, I can feel His presence, caring for me, loving me, working things out."

Elizabeth often experiences the reality of God in a kinesthetic sense, feeling, holding on to tangible proof of His care, sensing His physical presence beside her. She would identify with Psalm 73:23-25: "I am always with you; you hold me by my right hand. You guide me" (NIV).

The reality of Christ's presence

Pastor F. B. Meyer boarded a streetcar in north London and sat down in an empty seat. Opposite him sat a sad-faced elderly woman with a basket on her lap.

After a time, she spoke to him. "Pastor Meyer?"

"Yes. May I help you?" he asked.

"I've been a widow for a long time," she began. "My only companion has been my crippled daughter. She was such a joy to me. Every day when I came home from work, she welcomed me. Every night in the darkness I could reach over and touch her. But she died and I'm alone and miserable. I'm on my way home now, but it doesn't seem like home anymore, for she isn't there."

"The Lord will be there when you get home," Pastor Meyer said. "When you open the door, I want you to say out loud, 'Jesus, I'm home! I know You are here!' Then as you light the fire to fix supper, talk to Him about your day. Talk to Him just as you used to talk to your daughter. Then sit for a while, open His Word, and allow Him to speak to you. Then at night in the darkness, reach out your hand and say, 'Jesus, I know You are here beside me.' "

The streetcar reached the end of the line, and the pastor and the widow got off, going different directions.

Several months later, the pastor rode the same streetcar and was greeted by a cheerful woman whom he did not recognize.

"You don't remember me?" she asked. "I am that woman who missed her crippled daughter so much. We talked in this same streetcar a few months back."

"Ah, yes!" Pastor Meyer remembered. "And what happened?"

"I went home and did just as you told me to do. When I put my key in the lock, I called out, 'Jesus, I'm home!' Then as I fixed my supper, I talked out loud to Him and told Him all about my day. Then I sat for a while and read His Word and listened to Him speak to me. Then when I was in bed and the lights were out, I stretched out my hand in the darkness and said, 'Take my hand, Lord. I need to feel Your touch.' Now He has become my dear and constant Companion. What a difference He has made in my life!"[6]

Explore for yourself

1. Divide a sheet of paper into three sections. Label them Auditory, Visual, and Kinesthetic. In each section, make a list of Scripture verses that communicate in that particular learning style.

2. Try this auditory experiment. Make an acrostic using the letters of your entire name. Think of something you need from God that begins with each letter. Or let each letter begin a sentence of a prayer of praise and adoration.

3. The following psalms were acrostic poems based on the Hebrew alphabet: psalms 9, 10, 25, 34, 37, 112, 119, 145. Make your own acrostic prayer based upon your alphabet. Write a sentence or two that begins with each letter of the alphabet.

4. Try this visual experiment. Think of some of the buried hurts and resentments from the past. Make a list of all the wrongs you have stored up that still hurt when you think about them. When you are ready to give them up to God, to release yourself from them, to forgive that person as God has asked you to do, throw the paper in a fire, or set it on fire with a candle, and watch it burn.

5. Sketch a prayer. Stick figures and simple drawings will do fine. Draw some representation of what God means to you. Then depict yourself in relationship to God.

6. Try a kinesthetic experiment. Pick an object from nature, such as a tulip bulb. Ask God to give you a message through that object. Look at it; handle it; cut it open. What journey has it taken to be the object you see now? Have other forces affected it? What might it become? What does it tell you about yourself? Others? God? Can you think of a Bible verse that reinforces the message?

7. Take a prayer walk. Walk where you can feel free to talk aloud to God. Invite Christ to walk with you. Talk to Him about the happenings of your life. Sit on a log or bench, and ask the Lord to sit beside you. Share whatever is on your heart. You may want to divide your walk into four sections or to have four stopping places. During each section, pray one section of an ACTS prayer: Adoration, Confession, Thanksgiving, and Supplication.

Explore in a group

1. Have members of the group quote favorite Bible promises. Look at each promise to see whether it uses auditory, visual, or kinesthetic imagery.

2. Let each person in the group share times when God seems especially near to them. Listen to see whether their words are more auditory (*listen, hear, speak, tell*); visual (*see, show, look, observe, notice*); or kinesthetic (*feel, touch, taste, smell, handle, do*).

3. Give everyone an envelope containing ten toothpicks. Tell them to sit in silence for five minutes, thinking about what God means to them. They are then to use the toothpicks to express their relationship with God. They can break or bend the toothpicks. They may spell words or use them to form a picture.

After all are ready, go around the group, each sharing what he or she has tried to express with the toothpicks.

4. While soft music plays, ask the group to think back over their week. Where have they SEEN God at work in their lives? When did they HEAR the Holy Spirit speak? When did they FEEL God's touch? Share with the group.

4

Discovering Praise

All who seek the Lord shall find him and shall praise his name. Their hearts shall rejoice with everlasting joy (Psalm 22:26, TLB).

I stumbled out of bed to shut off my ringing alarm clock. My head ached, and I wanted nothing so much as to crawl back into bed and forget about going to work.

The day before had been a difficult one at school. I had driven home wondering how I'd ever survive until the end of the week, let alone the end of the school year. What had happened to my usual joy in teaching?

I looked in the mirror and didn't like what I saw! My hair needed a perm, and there were dark circles under my eyes. *I'm so tired, Lord,* I thought. *I don't want to go to school. I don't want to face any more problems. I just want to hibernate until next spring! If only I could teach in a different school where children were always cooperative and staff members never misunderstood.* I could hear raindrops pelting the windowpane. *Another rainy day when the children can't go outside to play. If only I lived in sunny Arizona instead of rainy British Columbia, things would be different!*

Still half asleep, I opened *Among Friends.* That morning's devotional thought was by my friend Ardis Stenbakken. She wrote, "Most people keep the same attitude no matter where they live or work or worship. The location isn't nearly as large a determinant as is attitude!"[1]

I woke up fast! Now, how was it possible that she would write just exactly what I needed to hear on that gloomy morning? "OK, Lord," I said. "I'll admit I need a change of attitude. I don't feel like it, but I'll try to think of things to praise You about as I drive to work this morning." From past experience, I knew that praise would drive away the dark clouds and bring me into the warmth of God's presence.

My mind was blank as I backed out of the garage and headed down the street. So I decided to use the letters of the word *praise* as an acrostic to get my mind in motion. Back at home that evening, I wrote the essence of the morning praise acrostic in my prayer journal.

P - Lord, I praise You for the **people** I work with. I praise You for the patience of Eleanor, the adaptability of Wayne, the cheerfulness of Karen, the creativity of Esmon, and the devotion of Joy. I thank You for the organization of Ian and the sensitivity of Pat, the humor of Byron and the thoughtfulness of Leise, the courage of Loney, the helpfulness of Tim, and the supportiveness of Kathy. (Already I was smiling, looking forward to meeting the other staff members.)

R - I praise You, Lord, for the promise of the **resurrection**. Because Jesus lives, my loved ones, too, shall live. Since Ron has gone to Bulgaria for eight weeks, I've been missing Mother and Daddy a lot. Because of Your resurrection, I have hope!

A - Lord, I praise You for **aromas** I enjoy. The delightful smells of baking bread, roses, scented bubble bath, the warm earth after a rain, wood smoke in the fall air, and the odor of fallen leaves along a woodland path.

I - Thank You, Lord, for **international** phone links that connect me with my husband in Europe and family members in the United States. What a comfort to know I can be connected with family by just lifting a receiver and punching a few buttons.

S - Lord, I praise You for **salvation**, for sending Your Son to

die for me and my children. Because of Your love, I can be saved from sin, from pain, from sorrow, and from all the troubles of this old world. Because of You, I have a way out!
E - Thank You, Lord, for **energy** to drive to work this morning, to face another day. Energize and empower me to represent You in my classroom.

It was surprising how uplifted I felt by the time I reached school. Forty-five minutes of praise had changed my attitude. It filled my heart to overflowing with joy! God seemed very close to me on that morning commute. All day I sensed His presence as I taught. Praise had brought me into God's presence and made a difference in my entire day!

The power of praise
In Psalm 22:3 David declares that God "inhabit[s] the praises of Israel" (NKJV). The New American Standard Bible says that God is "enthroned upon the praises of Israel." What an awesome thought that God literally dwells amid the praises of His people! He draws near to us when we praise Him! Our heartfelt words of praise bring us into His joyful, energizing presence!

Ellen White expressed the same idea when she said, "The soul may ascend nearer heaven on the wings of praise."[2]

In her book *Light in My Darkest Night*, Catherine Marshall tells of the "dark night of the soul" that she experienced after the death of her granddaughter. She shares how the sunlight of Christ's presence came to her when she began to praise Him in spite of how she felt.

Catherine learned to say with the psalmist, "My heart is fixed, O God, my heart is fixed: I will sing and give praise" (Psalm 57:7). It was not easy, but Catherine chose to make a sacrifice of praise (see Psalm 107:22).

She began to climb out of her dark valley the day she wrote in her journal, "The message to me yesterday was most specific. I am to arise each morning at 6:00 a.m. and rejoice in the Lord. I am to praise Him with a grateful heart. I am to pour out my love for Him. I am to thank Him for everything that has gone wrong in my life."

Reluctantly, Catherine began to look for ways to praise God. When no praise came to her mind, she simply read words of praise from the Psalms. For days, her praise seemed to her hollow and shallow and of no use at all.

Then one morning she wrote, "I feel a flutter in my spirit, Lord." A little later, she was able to say, "I am feeling Your presence again after so many months of darkness."

Soon after, she penned, "A feeling rises up inside me that little trickles of praise are now running together, merging, beginning to form a small river of praise. It began mechanically, yet now has increasingly the feel of spontaneous emotion."[3]

The power of praise had lifted Catherine Marshall out of the valley of despair and brought her into the very presence of Jesus.

She found God again when she discovered praise.

The results of praise

One morning I was struck by the connection between praise and the presence of Christ in the life when I read the following statement from the book *Christ's Object Lessons.*

If we keep the Lord ever before us, allowing our hearts to go out in thanksgiving and praise to Him, we shall have a continual freshness in our religious life. Our prayers will take the form of a conversation with God as we would talk with a friend. He will speak His mysteries to us personally. Often there will come to us a sweet joyful sense of the presence of Jesus.[4]

For some time, I thought about the four results that would come into my life when I offered praise to God.

1. I would have a continual freshness in my spiritual experience.

2. My prayers would become more like real conversations with a friend.

3. God would reveal His mysteries to me personally.

4. I would have a sweet, joyful sense of His presence.

Wow! I thought. *I've been missing a lot! I've got to praise God more!* I wrote in my journal:

> Lord, I feel like praising You this morning, immersing myself in the coolness of Your presence, allowing You to bring a new freshness and crispness to my wilted heart. I want to be like a stalk of limp celery crisping up in cold water!

I then wrote the following praise acrostic.

P - Lord, I praise You for the **purpose** You have for my life. I feel content this morning that Your purpose has been fulfilled in the way You have led in recent committees.

R - Lord, I praise You for Your **righteousness.** I accept Your righteousness this morning in place of my sin and unholiness. Cover me, forgive me, and bring me into a closer relationship with You.

A - I praise You, Lord, for Your **availability.** You are always there for me, available when I need You. You are always there to give me strength and hope.

I - Lord, I praise You for Your **infinity.** Everything I know comes to an end, everything but You and Your love. What a comfort to know that because of Your unending love, I will be able to experience forever.

S - I praise You for the **surety** of Your promises. Your Word is forever. What You say, You will do! I can put my trust in You completely.

E - Lord, You are the source of all **energy.** All power and warmth that keeps the universe in space, that allows all life to exist, that infuses me with new life and healing comes from You. Lord, I praise You for Your life-giving energy.

Yes, Lord, I praise You for Your **P**urpose, **R**ighteousness, **A**vailability, **I**nfinity, **S**urety, and **E**nergy. What a marvelous, praiseworthy God You are! I worship You and adore You!

The next few days were joyful ones as I experienced the presence of Christ through the power of praise.

The power of a song

The journey through the hill country of India was tiring. Pioneer missionary E. P. Scott trudged along the jungle path, unaware that he was being watched. Suddenly he was surrounded by a band of warriors from a remote hill tribe. Slowly they began to close in on him, their spears pointed at his heart.

Lord, help me! Pastor Scott prayed silently. *They are going to murder me unless You intervene.*

He had no weapons to defend himself. All he carried was a bag with a few clothes and a little food and his violin. His heart beat quicker as he thought of the violin. Perhaps it would distract them until he could think about what to do next. Slowly he set down his belongings, opened the case, and took out the violin and the bow.

Lifting the violin to his shoulder, he began to play and sing the first hymn that came to mind, "All Hail the Power of Jesus' Name." His eyes closed in prayer as he sang the words of praise, Scott felt the presence of the Lord giving him courage and strength.

By the time he reached verse three and the words "Let every kindred, every tribe, / On this terrestrial ball, / To Him all majesty ascribe," the missionary opened his eyes to find that all spears had been lowered. The men stood quietly listening. Some were weeping. Scott continued his song of praise.

After he finished the song, the warriors invited him to tell them more about Jesus. Scott spent the remainder of his life ministering among this tribal group, sharing with them the gospel.[5]

Such is the power of praise!

Explore for yourself

1. Write your own acrostic based on the word *praise*. For each letter of the word, think of something that begins with that letter for which you want to praise God.

2. Look in the index of the hymnal for songs of praise that begin with each letter of the word *praise*. Use one verse of each

song as your acrostic of praise. Read, write, or sing the praise songs as your offering of praise to God.

3. Make a sacrifice of praise to God. See Psalm 27:6; 107:22; 116:17. When things are going well, it is easy to praise God. Such praise is an offering but not a sacrifice. When bad things happen and our hearts are heavy, then our choice to praise is indeed a sacrifice of joy.

4. Make a quilt of thanksgiving. Take a square of white paper. Fold it in half vertically, then horizontally. Now fold it once diagonally. Open it, and you will have a square containing eight triangles. Inside each triangle, draw a sketch of one thing for which you are thankful. If you are a quilter, you may want to make a complete fabric quilt in which each block expresses your praise and thanksgiving. Read the book *The Quilt* by T. Davis Bum, Bethany House Publishers. It is a powerful book about praise.

5. Skip and praise. Put on some cheerful praise music, and skip around the house, letting the joy of the music fill your heart with thanksgiving. Try jumping rope, praising the Lord for one of His attributes each time your feet touch the ground! Skip down a country road, and imagine Jesus at the other end waiting for you.

6. Go through the alphabet, making a list of God's attributes that begin with each letter. For example, the letter *A*: accepting, amiable, all-powerful, almighty, amazing, abiding, able, absolute, admirable, affirming, Alpha, abundant, awesome. Focus on a different attribute of God for each day. Build your praise around that attribute. Find Bible verses that illuminate that quality. For ideas, see Dick Eastman's *A Celebration of Praise: Exciting Prospects for Extraordinary Praise,* Baker Book House, 1992.

7. Take a praise tour of your home. Go into each room, and praise the Lord. What activities go on there? Who uses that room? What do the mementos of the room suggest about a subject for praise? How has God been near to you in that room? What gifts from God are in that room?

8. Make a list of ten of God's attributes in one column. In a

parallel column, make a corresponding list of your own contrasting character traits. For instance: God is powerful, but I am weak. God is all-knowing, but I know so little. At the end of the exercise, write down what you think God is saying to you today. What do you want to say to Him?

Explore in a group

1. Divide into groups of three or four. Ask each group to appoint a scribe, who will need a pen and paper. Give them five to ten minutes to brainstorm about the attributes of God. Suggest that they make an alphabet and think of as many attributes as possible beginning with each letter. After an appropriate time, call the groups together, and begin to list attributes on a chart, pooling ideas from all the groups. You will be amazed at the large list you get!

Then have a prayer and praise time, each person praising God for different attributes that are especially meaningful to him or her. Ask each person to tell why he or she chose those attributes.

2. Go around the group, and let each share a time when they experienced the power of praise in their own lives. Perhaps it was a time when the clouds of discouragement lifted after they began to praise or a time when God seemed particularly close as they praised Him for some of the tough times in their life.

3. Ask each person to bring an object from home that reminds him or her of something for which he or she is thankful. Let them tell why. It might be car keys, and he could tell of God's protection in recent travels. It might be a wedding picture, and she is thankful for God's blessing on their marriage by seeing them through a difficult period.

5

Seeking Solitude

Be still, and know that I am God
(Psalm 46:10).

After two hectic weeks of camp pitch, camp meeting, and pastors' meetings, I needed quietness. I drove to a sparkling blue lake surrounded by snowcapped mountains, where I could be alone to immerse myself in the silence of God.

In the stillness I sketched the scene in my journal and then recorded the following:

> It's so quiet. As I listen, I hear the far-off drone of an airplane engine, then the hum of dragonfly wings. There is an occasional splash of fish jumping out of the still water, the faint rustle of aspen leaves and grasses at the water's edge. Ducks call from the far right side of the lake; a chickadee chirps to my left. A fly buzzes near my head. A family of fourteen mallards make only an occasional splash as they search for food not far away.
>
> I feel the warmth of the sun even though I am sheltered by trees along the shore. A breath of air stirs the pages of my journal and causes the fireweed nearby to sway and shimmer.
>
> The smell of fall is in the air. It is a ripe smell, a pungent, earthy smell.
>
> A small airplane roars across the lake toward where

I sit, skimming the tops of the trees, circling to the right. From some hidden spot in the grasses, a frog scolds the pilot for disturbing the peace.

Marsh grasses have gone to seed already, turning gold and bronze in the sun. The fireweed blooms are almost to the end of the stalk. Here and there, fireweed seed pods have split open, releasing the soft white cotton. Rose leaves have turned yellow and rust. Wine rose hips dangle among them. Birches and alders are splotched with yellow.

Far across the lake, the breeze has ruffled the water enough to catch the sunlight. It looks like a flock of a thousand silver-winged birds dancing on the surface of the blue lake.

Lord, thank You for this beauty. Let the calmness of the scene seep into my soul, taking away the stress and worry of my life, helping me to trust completely in You. I want to be as sensitive to Your voice as the aspen leaves are to the whisper of the wind.

That August afternoon I had left the campgrounds feeling frazzled, fragmented, and frustrated by the stresses of the previous two weeks. I returned feeling renewed, revitalized, and energized for the days ahead.

Empty pitchers, empty cups
In the words of Anne Morrow Lindbergh, we spill ourselves "away in driblets to the thirsty," seldom allowing ourselves "the time, the quiet, the peace, to let the pitcher fill up to the brim." She writes:

> We throw ourselves indiscriminately into commit-
> tees and causes. Not knowing how to feed the spirit, we
> try to muffle its demands in distractions. Instead of
> stilling the center, the axis of the wheel, we add more
> centrifugal activities to our lives—which tend to throw
> us off balance.[1]

We must take time to feed our spirits, to rediscover the springs of God's love that will fill our cups. For a little while each day, we need to "be still" and experience the presence of God, to really get to know Him as a friend. Solitude allows us freedom to listen to God's voice, to bask in the joy of His presence, to share with Him leisurely, and to receive His strength and power.

Steps into solitude

In his book *Celebration of Discipline,* Richard J. Foster suggests four steps we can take that will lead us to find a joyful experience with Christ in solitude.[2]

Step 1: Grab moments of solitude. He suggests such times as the early moments in bed before anyone else awakens, the time we spend waiting in offices or airports, the quiet we have while driving alone in bumper-to-bumper traffic, or those times when we lie awake in the night, unable to sleep.

Suzanna Wesley, mother of nineteen children, had the habit of pulling her apron over her head when she was communing with the Lord. Her children knew that when she did that, she needed to be alone with God. She was not to be disturbed.[3]

Evelyn Christenson, author of *What Happens When Women Pray,* remembers how she cherished the night feedings when her babies were small. With no other distractions, she spent the time in quiet meditation and prayer. Those times of solitude became precious because the presence of Christ became real in the silence.[4]

Recently I captured twenty minutes of solitude while waiting for the printers to finish worksheets I needed for a seminar. Instead of sitting in the shop, I returned to my car and asked the Lord to speak to me in the stillness.

My car faced an intersection known as Five Corners. While I watched the rhythm of the traffic passing the signals, the Lord seemed to speak to me through the scene. I wrote in my journal:

Lord, I need such clear signals for the traffic of thoughts and ideas that go buzzing around my mind. I need Your Holy Spirit to give me a kind of inner traffic-light system that signals what I should do next or how I should respond in a given situation.

Show me, Lord, when I should stop and proceed no farther! Help me to clearly see Your green light that says, "Go for it, Dorothy. Now is the time to move!" Help me to be aware of Your flashing yellow lights of caution in situations I face. Often I can't see the subtle implications of my actions.

Just as these lights have a left-turn arrow, help me to hear Your voice saying, "Turn right. Turn left. Go straight ahead!" Make me sensitive to Your Holy Spirit speaking to me.

Those few minutes of solitude calmed me and gave me strength to enter a time of intensive ministry at a women's retreat the following weekend. That night, the Lord awakened me, giving me yet more moments of solitude, during which I sensed a new direction I should take in leading the early-morning prayer session.

Step 2: Develop a quiet spot at home. My husband has his private sanctuary in a corner of the family room, where he has a mobile computer center turned into a study center. There, he keeps his notes, pens, Bibles, concordance, Greek lexicon, and other materials. I have a sanctuary in a chair on our sun porch with my devotional materials in a wicker basket. When we are in those spots, it is a signal that we desire solitude.

My friend Gloria Lindo has turned a spare bedroom into a prayer room. It is a small room of beauty and privacy with cushions and soft lighting that anyone can use as a prayer retreat.

Step 3: Withdraw for brief quarterly retreats. Foster suggests spending three or four hours once a quarter in total silence before the Lord. He suggests using this as a time for taking stock of life and evaluating your goals and objectives. Spend the time in prayer, asking God to help you dream and stretch your mind to encompass His will for your life in the weeks ahead.

Such retreats need to be spent absolutely alone, in total silence. Some can manage this during a morning at home. Others need to go to a park or church, take a long hike in the woods, stay late at the office, rent a motel room, or find a library carrel.

Be quiet and just let the Lord reveal Himself in the stillness. Have your Bible and notebook ready to use as He directs.

Step 4: Plan once-a-year study retreats. These retreats would again be done in solitude and silence for one day or perhaps a weekend. Like Jesus, we plan to withdraw from people and the hassles of life. We choose to be alone so that we can immerse ourselves in the silence of God and allow Him to speak to us through His Word.

So many voices clamor for our attention. There are voices of family, colleagues, and friends. We hear voices of pain, fear, anger, desire, and blame. There are haunting voices from our past, voices of parents, grandparents, teachers, and children. There are voices of the present duties, obligations, and problems to be solved. There are voices of the future speaking of plans, hopes, dreams, and opportunities.

We need times of silence and solitude when we can hush these voices. Only then can we hear God's voice, that still, small voice that Elijah heard while hiding in the cave. "When every other voice is hushed, and in quietness we wait before Him, the silence of the soul makes more distinct the voice of God."[5]

We are not naturally tuned to the still, small voice. We want God to speak to us in thunder tones from the pulpit. We long for the fireworks of God to shake us up and set us on the right path. Instead, He whispers to us, "Be still and know that I am God."

Reasons for solitude

It was Friday morning after an extra-busy week. I longed to stay in bed and be lazy for the day. I was too tired to even want to go birding or to read a good book, both activities I thoroughly enjoy. I was exhausted, burned out, and drained dry. When I finally struggled out of bed and opened my Bible, one verse stood out for me in bold letters because it spoke so directly to my need for silence and solitude.

The verse was Job 37:14: "Stop and consider God's wonders" (NIV).

"Right on, Lord!" I exclaimed with a smile. I drew a hexagonal stop sign in my journal and wrote the word *STOP* in capital letters. I laid aside the chores I had for the day and spent more than an hour looking up other references where the Lord tells us to stop! I discovered four reasons to stop.

1. Stop and listen to His voice (1 Samuel 9:27; Numbers 9:8).

Only as other voices are hushed can we hear His voice speaking. I wonder how many mistakes I have made because I haven't taken time to listen to His whispers of love.

2. Stop to watch for God's deliverance (Exodus 14:13; 2 Chronicles 20:17). We need to spend less time trying to figure out how to escape from the trials and difficulties of life and more time watching God work on our behalf. We need to stop depending on ourselves so that we can begin depending on Him.

3. Stop and get to know God (Psalm 46:10). Just as we need time alone to share with friends if we are to get to know each other, so we need time alone with God to truly get to know Him.

4. Stop and consider God's miracles (Job 37:14; 1 Samuel 12:16). It's good now and again to be quiet long enough to look back and remember where God has been working miracles in our lives. So often these wondrous works of God pass us by because we haven't stood still long enough to observe.

Sometimes those miracles come in the most unexpected places. Recently I arrived in Fayetteville, Arkansas, on my way to a prayer conference, only to discover that my luggage hadn't arrived. I decided to wait for the plane that was due an hour later.

While I waited to fill out my lost-luggage report, I looked up to see Merlin and Juanita Kretschmar standing at a nearby counter. After a quick greeting, they went to check in for their flight, and I stayed in line to report my missing baggage.

Once the report was filled out, I went to see if the Kretschmars had left. Their flight had been delayed, so we had a few minutes to talk. In that short time, Juanita gave her testimony of the miraculous way the Lord had recently led her and Merlin to a new ministry in the Florida Keys. We had prayer about my luggage and parted.

Later that evening in my quiet time, I suddenly realized what a miracle it was that we had met. Had my luggage arrived with me, I would have been gone before the Kretschmars got there. Had their plane left on time, we would not have had that moment to talk and pray together—and I needed the encouragement of that encounter. It was one of God's little miracles.

God is working miracles all the time in our lives. We need to stop often, spending time in solitude reviewing His wondrous works in our lives, listening to His voice, waiting for His direction, and strengthening our friendship.

Explore by yourself

1. Invest in a spiritual RRSP (Read, Reflect, Stillness, Pray). Read a short portion of Scripture, a psalm, or a story. Read it several times, perhaps in different Bible versions. Reflect on its meaning for your time and situation. What is God saying to you in this passage? Sit silently, asking God to speak to you anything He wants to say to you about your day or your situation. Talk over with the Lord what He has been telling you, and give Him your response and plan for the day.

2. Experiment with silence. Go for a whole day without speaking. (You may have to unplug the phone.) You need not withdraw from people, but just find other ways to relate to them. Record your feelings about the day. Savor the silence.

3. Find a corner of your home that can serve as a silent sanctuary. Have all of your devotional materials in one place on a special desk, shelf, basket, or table. Let others in your family know that you wish to be given an uninterrupted time of solitude when you are in that place.

4. Find a place of solitude where you can be away from people, telephones, television, radio, and recorded music for three or four hours. Immerse yourself in the silence of God. Ask Him to help you think of the ways He has blessed you during the past

week, month, or year. Become aware of how God has been working in your life. Or ask Him to put His dreams for the future within your mind. Write down what you think He wants you to do. Resist all stimulation except the sounds of nature and the words of Scripture.

5. Find a quiet spot in nature where you will not be interrupted. Write down everything you hear, taste, smell, see, and feel. What message is God speaking to your heart through your surroundings? "Christ is ever sending messages to those who listen for His voice."[6]

Explore in the group

1. Can you identify with the author's experience of several hours of solitude? Where were you? What benefits did you receive from spending the time alone in silence? Share with the group how you have reacted to times of intense quiet.

2. Discuss: What is the difference between loneliness and solitude? Do you agree with Henri Nouwen, who has said that "without solitude it is virtually impossible to lead a spiritual life"?[7] What are some of the things we let go of in times of solitude?

3. William Penn once said that solitude is "a school few care to learn in, tho' none instructs us better."[8] Think of Bible characters who spent times of solitude with God. For instance, Jesus, Elijah, Enoch, David, Paul, John, and Jeremiah all spent periods of solitude alone with God. What lessons did they learn in those times of chosen or enforced solitude? What lessons have you learned from your own times of solitude?

4. Give the group members ten minutes (or more) to spend in solitude. If possible, let each find a place away from all the others. Come together at a specified time and share. What difficulties did you face in hushing the heart? Did you gain any new insights into Scripture or your own life? What did the solitude teach you?

6

Finding Friendship

*You are my friends
(John 15:15, TLB).*

The year was 1844. Joseph Scriven stood alone on the deck of a ship bound for Montreal and stared at the rolling Atlantic Ocean. It was such dark waters that had snatched his sweetheart from him in an accidental drowning the day before their wedding was to have taken place in Dublin, Ireland.

The depth and breadth of his sorrow was like the ocean carrying him along to a new life in Canada. During that time of great personal sorrow, the only thing that kept Joseph afloat was the comfort of Jesus Christ, his personal Saviour and Friend.

Joseph settled in Port Hope, Ontario. He took seriously the words of John 15:14: "You are my friends if you do whatsoever I command you." Trying to practice the words of Jesus in the Sermon on the Mount, Joseph gave freely of his possessions, sometimes taking the clothes off his back for someone in need. Everyone in that town knew that Joseph Scriven was a friend of Jesus.

One man, on seeing Joseph walking the streets of the town carrying a sawhorse, said, "I'd like to have that man work for me."

"You'll never get Joseph to work for you," someone replied. "He saws wood only for poor widows and sick people who can't pay."

Thirteen years after Joseph left Ireland, he received word that his mother was seriously ill. Unable to go to her, he did the next best thing—he wrote her a letter, enclosing a poem he had written for her.

> Have we trials and temptations?
> Is there trouble anywhere?
> We should never be discouraged;
> Take it to the Lord in prayer!

It is evident that the words came out of his own experience of sorrow and finding in Jesus a Friend who was always there to give comfort and encouragement.

> Can we find a friend so faithful,
> Who will all our sorrows share?
> Jesus knows our every weakness;
> Take it to the Lord in prayer!

Later, when Joseph himself was sick, a friend came to visit and discovered the poem. "Did you write this?" he asked.

"The Lord and I did it between us," Joseph replied. That poem was later set to music and is found in many hymnals under the title "What a Friend We Have in Jesus."[1]

Friendship with God

"What is your greatest spiritual asset?" an interviewer asked Dr. John D. Adams. He expected that it might be the man's extensive library or his hard-earned degree.

"My consciousness of the actual presence of Jesus," Dr. Adams replied. "Nothing bears me up so as the realization that Jesus is always with me in actual presence. Christ is the home of my thoughts. Whenever my mind is free from other matters, it turns to Christ, and I talk aloud to Him when I am alone—on the street, anywhere—as easily as to a human friend."[2]

Ellen White would agree. Friendship with God is a theme found throughout her writings. In Steps to Christ she says, "We may keep so near to God that in every unexpected trial our thoughts will turn to Him as naturally as the flower turns to the sun."[3]

For this friendship with God to become a reality, we must do more than read about Him, listen to sermons about Him, and meditate upon His wondrous works. "In order to commune with God, we must have something to say to Him concerning our actual life."[4]

* Just as we share intimately with our dearest human friends about the happenings and concerns of our lives, so we are to keep our wants, our joys, our sorrows, our cares, and our fears before God. We cannot burden Him. We cannot weary Him.[5]

The ultimate Friend

It's astonishing that "the relations between God and each soul are as distinct and full as though there were not another soul upon the earth to share His watchcare."[6] It seems incredible that the almighty God of the universe; His Son, Jesus Christ; and the Holy Spirit want to relate to me as to a friend!

In his book *Making Real Friends in a Phony World,* Jim Conway lists the following description of true friends. They are nonjudgmental, caring, accepting, trusting, committed, genuine, self-disclosing, enabling, spiritually concerned, and firm.[7] There's no doubt about it; all of those characteristics apply to God!

A two-way street

However, friendship is a two-way street. Not only is God our Friend; He wants us to be His friends too. The same skills that will help us make friends with our peers will help us to be friends of God.

We were created to be God's friends, and He is longing for us to relate to Him with acceptance, listening, affirmation, and trust. He hopes that we will choose to love Him, to share ourselves honestly with Him, and to be loyal to Him.

Prayer is where the communication of friendship with God takes place. It is our opportunity not only to receive the blessings of His friendship, but to return to God our love, trust, affirmation, and loyalty.

Morning visit with a friend
It was a glorious April morning in the Fraser Valley of British Columbia, Canada. I opened the sliding doors of our sun room to let in the sights, sounds, and smells of spring. The song of a redwing echoed my sense of wonder and joy. I listened to the happy chirps of sparrows, finches, juncos, and chickadees at the three feeders in my garden.

It had rained during the night, leaving diamondlike droplets hanging from pine needles and sitting on pansy petals. The bright blues of grape hyacinths contrasting with the brilliant gold of forsythia was like a picture out of *Ideals* magazine.

The delicate perfume of violets and pansies mingled with the luscious scent of wet soil and growing things. A whiff of warm toast from the neighbor's kitchen drifted in.

God seemed so real to me that spring morning that I imagined Him sitting across the table from me as though He were a neighbor who had just dropped in for a cup of herb tea.

His hands lay upon the table—strong, work-worn hands. I imagined Him with black hair, Jewish face with a long nose, and a swarthy complexion. His eyes searched my face with understanding, and He smiled His acceptance of me, just as I was, in blue jeans, sweat shirt, and running shoes.

I imagined Him in white. His clothes were clean and pressed, and I wondered who did His laundry. Who did it when He was on earth? Women, of course, women who loved Him. What a neat thought! Had I been living then, I would gladly have washed His dusty clothes and hung them on my line to dry.

I sat there for a while, enjoying the warmth of His presence, listening to Him speaking to my heart. I recorded in my journal the silent exchange we had that morning.

"How are you, Dorothy?" He asks.

"I don't have much of a headache this morning. My left shoulder muscles hurt a little, but all in all I feel pretty good. I'm just glad to be alive! I'm so thankful You are helping me lose weight. I'm grateful for the way You've been working to bring healing to me after my cancer surgery last summer. I feel so much better than I did a year ago! I praise You, Lord!"

"What are your plans for today?"

"I need to outline topics for the prayer conference. Lord, I do need Your guidance in this. Help me, please, to be sensitive to Your leading. I want these talks to be a blessing, to give Your message.

"And that's not all. I have a box of correspondence to care for and two boxes of filing to do. I also thought I'd go shopping. I need some new Sabbath clothes."

"It sounds like a lot, Dorothy." He speaks with understanding. "Don't get frustrated if you can't do it all. In the light of eternity, how important are the items on your to-do list? Pause now and again to enjoy the world I've made for you. Stop occasionally to talk to Me. Just remember that I will be with you every moment of the day and that I love you. I will bless you today if you will let Me do it. I don't mean one blessing now, as you begin your day, but many little blessings to bring you renewed strength and energy throughout the day.

"So please don't forget Me, Dorothy, in your rush to finish your list of things to do. I'm here! I'm with you. I'll help you. I'm your Friend."

My mind turned immediately to the promise of Isaiah 41:10: "Do not fear, for I am with you; do not be dismayed, for I am your God. I will strengthen you and help you" (NIV).

The memory of that time with my Friend went with me all day. My work seemed light and my chores easy. That morning I had found it true that "prayer is the opening of the heart to God as to a friend."[8]

Explore it yourself

1. If Christ were living on earth today and you could invite Him to your house for a visit, what would you say to Him? Revelation 3:20 tells us that He is standing at the door of our lives, knocking, wanting to come in and sit at our tables with us

and share in our lives. Try the experiment the author described above. Write out your conversation with God. What do you say to Him? Listen for what He says to you. You will know that His message is true when it agrees with His message in Scripture.

2. Abraham was known as "a friend of God." Read again Abraham's experience in Scripture and in the book *Patriarchs and Prophets*, pages 125-170. Make a list of the reasons why he was known as God's friend. What qualities of a true friend did he exhibit in his relationship with God?

3. Read the chapter "The Privilege of Prayer" in the book *Steps to Christ*. Then write a letter to God, sharing yourself completely with Him as you would with a dear friend. Write at least one paragraph for each of the following categories: wants, joys, sorrows, cares, and fears.

4. Try writing out in detail one of the darkest chapters of your life. Give it to your Friend, and ask Him to show you where He was at this time in your life and what He wants to do for you now.

5. Try a snapshot prayer. Try to think of a typical picture that might be taken of you at work. Imagine yourself at your computer, at the bedside of a patient, in the laboratory, on the tractor, or underneath a car, doing repairs. Look at the things in your hand, the people around you, the tasks you have to do. Try to picture Christ's presence in the picture, standing by your side. What do you want to say to Him about your work? What do you think He might say to you?

Explore in a group

1. While soft music is playing, meditate for a few moments about the friendship of Christ. How has He manifest the qualities of friendship to you: acceptance, caring, forgiveness, understanding, sharing, listening, affirmation, trustworthiness, self-disclosure, encouragement, empowerment, and loyalty? Share with the group specific incidents that have illustrated Christ's friendship in one of these areas.

2. In her book *Alone With God*, Matilda Erickson Andross says that "The sentence 'Jesus and I are friends' contains the

secret of the Christian life; and every Christian has the privilege of finding in Jesus a real personal friend."[9] Do you agree or disagree? What is the basis for your conclusion?

3. What prevents us from having a close, personal friendship with Jesus? What do we need to do to make this companionship with God a daily reality? You may want to do some research in the Spirit of Prophecy. Check the index under "communion: with Christ and with God" and "companionship."

4. Share one practical step you plan to take during the next week to strengthen your friendship with God.

PART TWO

Exploring Personal Prayer

Getting Guidance

You will hear a Voice behind you say, "No, this is the way; walk here" (Isaiah 30:21, TLB).

On April 18, 1906, the city of San Francisco was awakened at five-fifteen to the sound of screams, windows rattling, and buildings crumbling.

The bewildered students of a girls' boarding school stumbled to the head of a wide stairway, where the matron stood at the bottom, waiting to give directions.

"Come down quickly and march along the hall to the vacant lot across the street," she commanded.

The frightened girls clutched one another's hands and began to descend the trembling stairs.

As the matron waited, an inner voice spoke to her clearly, "No! They must not come down!"

"Stop!" the matron screamed above the rumble of the quake. "Do not come down. Stay where you are!" Moments later, the entire front wall of the building collapsed outward, across the street where the girls would have been. Had they followed the matron's original orders, they would all have been killed.[1]

Directions from God

A multitude of Christians through the ages could tell similar stories of God's giving direction to their lives.

Nineteen-year-old Leonard Lee was running away from God when he was caught in a blizzard so intense he could not see a foot ahead of him. He plodded on, not daring to stop. Three times when he turned to the right, he heard a voice speak his name and say, "Turn to the left!" He obeyed and was led to a cabin where an injured trapper had been praying for help. Because Leonard listened to God's voice, he saved the life of the trapper as well as his own.[2]

Ejnar Lundby intended to cancel his sermon in an Oslo church to be with a man who was to be executed the next day for a murder he did not commit. As he reached for the phone to cancel, an inner voice said, "No! You must go to that meeting!" He obeyed, but instead of his prepared sermon, he shared the story of the innocent man, Kristian. After the meeting, the only living person who was in on the crime met Ejnar at the door.

The witness signed a statement, and Ejnar took it to the home of the state prosecutor. The execution was postponed, the witness testified, and Kristian was released from prison.

About this experience, Dr. Lundby says, "Every day I take time to pray and then to quietly wait for God to speak. Whenever I hear that silent, inner voice giving me direction, I try to obey immediately. In this way God has led me to some really exciting adventures for Him."[3]

Listening to God

"I have not met many who know how to listen to God," writes Gordon MacDonald in *Ordering Your Private World.* "Most Christians learned at an early age how to talk to God, but they did not learn to listen as well."[4]

Judith C. Lechman suggests a number of ways God speaks to us. He speaks in Scripture, devotional literature, other people's words and actions, the seemingly unimportant events of our daily lives, the tragedies and achievements of life, the wonders of nature, and by an inner voice in the silence of our souls.[5]

One way we can sensitize ourselves to hear God's voice speaking to us in our daily lives is to keep a spiritual journal.

Not long ago, I was looking for something in my journals, and in the process I read through several of them. It was exciting to see how God had almost imperceptibly been speaking to me, directing what I should do and how I should deal with certain situations. The pattern of His leading was apparent, and I couldn't wait to tell my husband my new insight. "My journals are better than a novel!" I exclaimed. "I can see how He has been at work in our lives, and it is just so exciting!"

Amy Carmichael, David Brainerd, Anne Morrow Lindbergh, John Wesley, George Whitefield, Blaise Pascal, Thomas Merton, David Livingstone, and Francis Asbury are a few famous Christians who have kept spiritual journals. Bill Hybels, Richard C. Foster, Becky Tirabassi, Gordon MacDonald, and Dwight Nelson are contemporary Christian writers who record God's guidance in spiritual journals.

Is it really God's voice?

"Christ is ever sending messages to those who listen for His voice,"[6] is the message I copied one morning. I then wrote:

> Lord, tune my ears and heart to hear Your voice. In the past I have made needless mistakes because I rushed on to do without first hearing what You would have me do. How foolish. Today, I will listen for Your will for my life.

Since then, I've thought a lot about listening to God's voice. How can I know it is really God speaking—and not Satan or my own wishful thinking? Are there some guidelines I should follow in trying to decipher His voice?

In his book *How to Listen to God,* Charles Stanley suggests some Biblical guidelines:[7]

1. The message will be consistent with Scripture(Isaiah 8:20). It is the devil, not the Lord, speaking when the voice tells us that our sins are too great for God to forgive or that it is OK for us to commit adultery in our circumstances. Both contradict the written Word of God.

2. The message may conflict with human wisdom(Isaiah 55:8). A lot of things God may ask us to do may not make sense from our vantage point; they may not be what we desire at all.

God often surprises us with His wisdom.

3. The message will clash with our carnal natures (Galatians 5:16-25). The work of the Holy Spirit is to draw us away from gratification of fleshly lusts. He will never lead us to satisfy discord, hatred, selfish ambition, jealousy, drunkenness, or immoral desires. The cult members who testified that God told them to kill were hearing another voice, not the Holy Spirit.

4. It will call for faith, courage, and patience (Psalm 27:14; Joshua 1:9; Hebrews 11). God's way is seldom the easy way. It is Satan who urges us to rush into a decision without proper consideration of the consequences.

5. We will have peace about the decision (Colossians 3:15). Until the Lord leads us to have settled peace that it is indeed His voice, we should proceed with caution. God will never give us peace about a path of disobedience to His revealed Word.

6. The longer we have known God, the easier it is to recognize His voice (John 10:4). Those who are beginning their Christian walk would do well to counsel with someone they respect who has had much experience in recognizing God's voice.

A recent example

For several weeks, I had been asking God's guidance about what writing project I should do next. I had four different ones in mind and had been filling file boxes with materials for each of the topics. As the time drew near that I had blocked off to write up a book proposal, I pretty well had made up my mind on one topic.

The day came on my calendar when I was to begin writing the proposal, but other urgent matters intruded. Anyway, I was having doubts whether I should do that topic. The next day, still thinking of that one topic, I prayed for guidance before turning on the computer.

During Bible study, the Lord focused my mind on John 21:6: "Throw your net on the right side of the boat" (NIV). I wrote,

"Lord, help me to hear Your voice when it says, 'Throw your net on the other side.' "

I turned on the computer and looked at my notes for the topic I had chosen. The ideas just weren't fitting together.

"Throw your net on the other side," an inner voice whispered. I took out my file on prayer. The outline rapidly began to fit together. In less than half the time I'd expected, I had a proposal in the mail for this book. Five days later, I had a call from Pacific Press editor Jerry Thomas. "Yes, we want *Prayer Treasures*," he said. "How soon can you get it to us?"

Looking back through my journals, I can see clearly how the Lord was speaking to me about this book for more than a year, leading me to topics, giving me fresh experiences in prayer, and giving me the ideas I would need when the time came to write.

The day I mailed the proposal, I felt blessed by Psalm 139:3: "You chart the path ahead of me, and tell me where to stop and rest. Every moment, you know where I am" (TLB). I wrote:

> What a precious thought. I may not know where I'm going, but You do, Lord. Thank You for that assurance. Help me to be always sensitive to Your guiding me in the way You would have me go.

The same yesterday, today, and forever

The Sabbath School lesson that week was about how God had directed Philip to the chariot of the Ethiopian court official. The class discussion in Clarkston led to the question "Why doesn't God speak to us now in miraculous ways as He did then?"

"Given the need and the circumstances, I believe He could and would, now as then," answered W. K. Reichard.

The next day while visiting friends, Reichard was suddenly aware of a quiet voice in his heart saying, "Go over to Lewiston."

It was dark when he reached Main Street in Lewiston, Idaho. He headed for the home of the only people he knew in town. They weren't home. He wandered around for a while, then headed home.

The voice spoke again, "Go to Main Street." The street was

deserted except for a darkened car with its engine running. A man was lying on the front seat.

Carbon monoxide! Reichard thought. He ran a block and a half to the nearest phone and called the police. Two patrol cars, lights flashing, rushed to the scene. Soon one sped the man to the hospital emergency room.

The policeman left behind to lock the man's car told Reichard, "You just saved a man's life!"

About that incident, Reichard wrote, "[That man] probably needed a few more years. And the Sabbath School class needed the certainty that God is the same, yesterday, today, and forever."[8]

Explore for yourself

1. Do a Bible study on guidance. Using a concordance, look up all the times the word *guide* is used. What do these verses tell you about God's willingness to give direction to your life?

2. Look up the words *guide* and *guidance* in the *Index to the Writings of Ellen G. White.* Make a chart of the major concepts covered. Read further on those areas that interest you most.

3. Choose a book of the Bible. Read through it, marking in green each passage in which God speaks personally to you, asking you to do something. Mark in red the passages in which He promises He will do something for you. Paraphrase the passages, using your name in the verses. Write out each verse in your journal. How does that verse apply to your daily life? What is God telling you to do?

4. Make a list of issues for which you seek God's guidance. Think ahead for the next week, month, or year. What are decisions that you will need to make? Give this list to God, asking Him to use whatever methods He chooses to guide you. Watch Him work to bring people, information, and circumstances together.

Explore in a group

1. Spend a few moments in quiet reflection about your life. Can you think of times when you heard God speaking a special

message to you in Scripture or when you sensed His direct guidance in a decision you had to make? Share one of those times with the group.

2. Perhaps some have had experiences when they thought something was of the Lord but discovered later that it was not His voice. Can they see where they went wrong? Why was it difficult to know for sure if it was God's leading? How could they have protected themselves against that error?

3. Make a list of Bible characters who received guidance from the Lord. How did God indicate His will to them? Can you think of some characters who followed the wrong voice? Why?

4. Divide into groups of three. Share one area in your life in which you need guidance. Discuss some of the pros and cons of the decision and your difficulty in knowing the right thing to do. Pray for one another that the Lord will give direction and will make you able to discern His voice when He speaks.

8

Finding Grace

Let us then approach the throne of grace with confidence, so we may receive mercy and find grace to help us in our time of need (Hebrews 4:16, NIV).

William Herschel, the great English astronomer, lived in constant fear of discovery for deserting the king's guards when he was seventeen. The penalty for desertion was death. After years of successfully avoiding capture, he received a summons to Windsor Castle to present himself before King George III.

Oh no! I've been found out! I will surely be exposed and thrown into prison to await execution! he thought. It was with quivering knees that he approached the throne.

King George smiled as William approached. "Before we discuss astronomy," the king said, "there is a little matter of business that we must attend to." With that, he handed William a document containing the king's seal and signature.

Fearfully, William opened the document. It was a pardon for his desertion! He no longer had to hide. He no longer faced death from his crime, for the king had offered him grace.[1]

What is grace?

Grace is favor that is undeserved; it is the gift of mercy in the place of punishment.

A woman once approached Emperor Napoleon with the request "Please pardon my son."

"No!" Napoleon replied. "This is your son's second offense. Justice demands his death."

"I don't ask for justice," the mother cried. "I plead for mercy."

"After the crime he's committed, he doesn't deserve mercy," Napoleon replied.

"If he deserved it, then it would no longer be mercy," she said. "Mercy is all I ask."

Moved by the mother's simple plea, the emperor declared, "Well, then I will have mercy. Your son is pardoned!"[2]

Grace is a king granting pardon. It is a father running to meet the prodigal. It is a mother's kiss when a child has been naughty. It is a gift presented to an undeserving, ungrateful friend.

Grace is an unmerited, undeserved, and unexpected favor given to an unworthy person. It is the lavish gift God extends to us as we approach His throne with guilty hearts. It is the amazing message that He is for us, not against us!

Often in prayer I have found the treasure of God's grace. As I have approached His throne, feeling foolish and guilty, He has smiled on me with favor and lovingkindness that I didn't deserve.

One morning I awoke at four o'clock and couldn't go back to sleep. All my mistakes of the past, my imperfections of character, and the many times I had failed God kept replaying in my mind until I felt completely discouraged. At last I got up and began reading in *The Ministry of Healing* where I had left off the day before. One of the texts quoted was Micah 7:18, 19. After reading it in several versions, I wrote my own paraphrase:

> Who is God like You who pardons my sins and forgives all my mistakes! You aren't angry with me, but You love me tenderly. You do not bring up my sins and failings, but You have thrown them far away from You, into the bottom of the sea, where they will never be found again!
>
> Lord, thank You! Help me do the same! Satan keeps trying to dig them up and bring them to mind. Help me

to accept Your love and forgiveness. Lord, please, You've blotted my sins from Your records, but they are still in the computer chips of my mind. Please blot them out there too!

Often in the simplicity of a little child I allow myself "to be gathered up in the arms of the Father," to "let him sing his love song" to me (Isaiah 43:4).[3] That morning, He quieted me with His love and grace (see Zephaniah 3:17).

Sometimes He gives His grace when I don't even ask for it!

One Friday afternoon after mailing letters and taking four hundred dollars cash from the bank, I went to the service station to get gas. Laying my purse on top of the car, I lifted the pump handle, but nothing happened.

The clerk came out of the store to announce, "Sorry, but our computer is down. Nothing works. I don't know how long it'll be."

I jumped into the car and zipped down half a block to another station. Finding that the pumps worked on the insertion of a credit card, I reached in the car for my purse. No purse! Then I remembered. I'd put it on top of the car at the other gas station, and it wasn't on top of the car now!

God, help me find that purse! I prayed as I jumped into the car and pulled into the line of traffic, looking along the road for my purse. It wasn't there, nor was it near the pumps of the first gas station.

I ran inside to ask the clerk, "Did anyone bring in a purse? I had it on top of my car when I left here a minute ago."

She shook her head. "Sorry, but no one brought one in. I'll ask the other clerk when she comes in."

I didn't wait but ran outside to find her. At that moment, I saw a woman run across the street toward the store, my purse in her hand. "Look what I found on the road!" she called to a woman pumping gas. "Someone must have dropped it!"

"You found it! You found it!" I gasped. "Thank you! Thank you so much!" I cried and gave her a big hug.

I offered a reward, but the woman refused. She was an off-duty employee of the store. "Just come back here and give us your business," she replied graciously.

I wrote a prayer of thanks for God's mercy in my journal that evening:

> That was so close! In the purse were over five hundred dollars, all my credit cards, driver's license, and passport. Thank You, precious Lord, for coming to my aid and not letting me suffer the results of my own stupidity. You treat me so much better than I deserve! How I love You and praise You for Your grace to me today!

The throne of grace

When we approach the throne of grace in prayer, we do not go alone. Jesus walks with us to the throne. He introduces us to God as His sons and daughters, members of the royal family, children of the heavenly King! He speaks on our behalf, presenting our requests as His own request.

When we kneel before God, Jesus kneels there with us. And we are told that when this happens, God the Father "lays open all the treasures of His grace" to us. We leave His presence knowing that He has answered our prayers and has filled our hearts with "the riches of His grace."[4]

Richard J. Foster expresses the same idea in his book *Prayer.*

> The truth of the matter is, we all come to prayer with a tangled mass of motives—altruistic *and* selfish, merciful *and* hateful, loving *and* bitter. Frankly, this side of eternity we will *never* unravel the good from the bad, the pure from the impure. But what I have come to see is that God is big enough to receive us with all our mixture. We do not have to be bright, or pure, or filled with faith, or anything. That is what grace means, and not only are we saved by grace, we live by it as well. And we pray by it.[5]

Isn't grace wonderful? Even when we pray, God's grace is at work, granting us special favor through the merits of Jesus Christ!

Recently my husband took some United States dollar checks to deposit in a Canadian bank. The teller told him she would have to charge him a dollar and a half for processing each one.

"I'll take them to another bank," Ron said.

At that moment, she looked at his account information that had come up on the monitor. "Oh, I'm sorry," she apologized. "I didn't realize yours is a Peak Performance Account. There will be no charge!"

I like to think something like that happens when I go to God in prayer. I have a Peak Performance Prayer Account because of my Friend Jesus, who goes with me to the throne!

One morning after meditating on God's marvelous grace, I wrote a prayer of gratefulness for what I saw:

G - Gentleness. Your grace is gentle, Lord. How tender-hearted You are! You are gentle with my fragile emotions, never bruising an already wounded spirit. You nudge me ever so softly toward the way You want me to go. Your grace is gentle.

R - Refreshing. Your grace is refreshing. Like the dew of the morning or a gentle summer rain, it gives me life and new hope. It is reviving and revitalizing. Your grace refreshes me!

A - Acceptance. Your grace is accepting. No matter how I have failed You, You don't throw me away. I feel totally accepted in Your presence, all I am, my strengths and weaknesses, my possibilities and my failures. Your grace accepts me.

C - Comfort. Your grace comforts me. In all the disappointments of life, even those of my own making, You comfort me. Your presence soothes, rubs salve into my wounded spirit, heals, and blesses me. Your grace is my comfort!

E - Encouragement. How You encourage me by Your unmerited love and favor! What joy and hope I have because of You and the gift of Your Son Jesus. If He died for me, He will surely save me and see me through all

the trials of life! Your grace encourages me!
Lord, this morning I praise You for Your **G**entle, **R**efreshing, **A**ccepting, **C**omforting, **E**ncouraging **GRACE.**

Explore for yourself

1. Do a study on the word *grace*. Each day, choose a different text where the word appears. Read it in context. Look up any cross references. Read it in several versions. Write your own paraphrase of the verse, inserting your name. Here are some texts to get you started: Romans 3:24; Galatians 1:6; Ephesians 2:8; 1 Peter 3:7; Psalm 84:11; Romans 5:20; 1 Corinthians 15:10; 2 Corinthians 12:9; 2 Peter 3:18.

2. In what areas of your life do you need to experience the favor and mercy of God? Write out a prayer giving each area of your life to God, asking Him to forgive you, accept you, and give you the riches of His grace for each situation.

3. Read the chapter "The Privilege of Prayer" in the book *Steps to Christ.* Find at least five reasons why we should "come boldly before the throne of grace." What arguments do we have that should give us courage to pray with confidence?

4. Use a tape recorder to record an oral confession of sins of the day, the week, or any time in the past. Confess that you are a sinner, and ask God to forgive you and blot out your sins from His record. Read the following texts: 1 John 1:9; Isaiah 1:18; Micah 7:18, 19; Psalm 79:8, 9. With those texts in mind, erase your confession. God has promised to blot out your iniquities and to remember your sins no more. Praise God!

5. Sing "Amazing Grace." What is the message of the song to your heart? What memories does it have for you? Read the story of how it was written in *Companion to the Seventh-day Adventist Hymnal.*[6] Try to find a biography or biographical sketch of John Newton. How does this song reflect the story of his life?

6. Write a love letter to God in response to your experience of His mercy and grace.

7. Write another verse for "Amazing Grace." Let it tell about your own personal experience with God's grace.

Explore in a group

1. Divide into groups of three or four. Work together to write an acrostic about what the word *grace* means in the life of a Christian. Share the acrostic. Or form an acrostic on the letters of the one who made grace possible, Jesus Christ.

2. Go around the circle, sharing a time when you experienced God's undeserved blessing, His gracious forgiveness, or His deliverance from danger. Then have a season of prayer to praise God for His mercy and lovingkindness to all present.

3. Allow ten to twenty minutes of quiet time for members of the group to write love letters to God, appreciating His goodness and mercy in their lives. Allow time for those who are willing to share their letters, or portions from them.

9

Visioning Victory

Thanks be to God! He gives us the victory through our Lord Jesus Christ (1 Corinthians 15:57, NIV).

Her head down, Elizabeth Mittelstaedt walked slowly onto a bridge near Frankfurt, Germany. She stood for a while, looking at the water splash over the rocks beneath her and thinking of the hopelessness of her life.

Elizabeth was in constant pain as the result of severe nerve and jaw damage during a routine dental procedure. Added to this was the emotional pain of her inability to have children.

I should jump into the river and put an end to my misery, Elizabeth thought. *What is the use of living?*

"Go ahead! Jump!" a voice said to her.

She looked again at the water and thought, *But it isn't deep enough to drown in!*

"Go ahead and jump! You'll hit your head on the rocks. That will kill you," the voice whispered.

That's Satan's voice! Elizabeth suddenly realized. *He's trying to tempt me just as he did Jesus when He stood on the pinnacle of the temple. Jesus didn't give in to Satan, and I don't have to give in to him either! I will not jump; I'll trust God instead.*

She began to cry as she poured out her heart to God. "Lord, I'm so afraid of living with this pain for the rest of my life. I don't know what to do. I don't think I can handle it. Help me!"

This time, Elizabeth heard another voice whisper to her, "Take no thought for the morrow; for the morrow shall take thought for the things of itself. Sufficient unto the day is the evil thereof."

"OK, Lord," she said. "You have told me not to worry about tomorrow. You'll give me strength for one day at a time. Today, I will trust You and not be afraid. Help me make it through today."

Elizabeth turned, then, and walked home, her head now held high. She knew that she had faced the enemy on the bridge that day and had gained the victory. Her weapons had been the Word of God and the prayer of faith in Jesus Christ.[1]

The sword of the Spirit

The Word of God is one of the weapons Paul recommended to the Ephesians (see Ephesians 6). This weapon, which Christ used to battle Satan, is just as effective today as it was then. In commenting on Christ's temptation in the wilderness, Ellen White wrote:

> Often the tempter comes to us as he came to Christ, arraying before us our weakness and infirmities. He hopes to discourage the soul, and to break our hold on God. Then he is sure of his prey. If we would meet him as Jesus did [with the words of Scripture], we should escape many a defeat.[2]

Mosquito battle

One brilliant June day in Alaska, I took a walk in the woods behind our house. I stopped at a fallen log to enjoy the wild-flowers—dwarf dogwood, pink wintergreen, and delicate twin flowers. Bright spots of wild rose bloomed along edges of the clearing. *What peace! What a paradise!* I mused. *I could stay here forever!*

Not quite! Within seconds, I was surrounded by a cloud of mosquitoes, huge, Alaskan-sized ones! I literally breathed them, getting one stuck in my throat!

Six mosquitoes zoomed in to land on the same spot on my bare hand. Within half an inch of the skin, they hovered a moment like tiny helicopters, then whirled away from that awful smell of Off!, a deep-woods mosquito repellant. Dozens more landed on my knees. I killed them with a swat of my hand, and immediately a dozen more moved in to take their places.

How much like life! I thought. *Satan sends in hundreds of temptations each day. I can expend my energy striking out at them, but each time I conquer one, the devil sends another to take its place. I cannot get rid of sin, evil, and temptation, any more than I can get rid of mosquitoes. But I can so saturate my mind with the Word of God that when Satan's dive bombers come in, they smell God's "Off!" There's no way they'll land when they sense the presence of Jesus covering me, protecting me!*

I thought of the words of the psalmist, "Your word have I hidden in my heart, that I might not sin against You!" (Psalm 119:11, NKJV).

In my journal that morning, I wrote:

> Lord, earth is no paradise, as beautiful as it may seem. Those pesky problems of sin spoil it all. Now I can do one of three things. I can sit still and let Satan have a feast, I can strike out and do battle with the devil, or I can take time to cover myself with Your Word!
>
> Help me to do the only sensible thing. Lord, help me to spend time with You and Your Word every day! Cover me with Your presence so that when Satan gets near, he'll smell You and go away!

The shield of faith

Prayer is the hand that grips the shield of faith. Without it, we are left defenseless. "No man is safe for a day or an hour without prayer."[3] It "is heaven's ordained means of success in the conflict with sin."[4]

"Satan cannot endure to have his powerful rival appealed to, for he fears and trembles before His strength and majesty. At the sound of fervent prayer, Satan's whole host trembles," says Ellen White.[5]

Samuel Chadwick writes:

Satan dreads nothing but prayer. The one concern of the devil is to keep the saints from praying. He fears nothing from prayerless studies, prayerless work, prayerless religion. He laughs at our toil, mocks at our wisdom, but trembles when we pray.[6]

Once in a while, God allows the veil that separates us from the invisible world to be drawn back so we can sense the reality of the forces of evil that would destroy us. He wants us to understand that we "wrestle not against flesh and blood, but against principalities, against powers, . . . against spiritual wickedness in high places" (Ephesians 6:12). He allows us to witness Satan trembling so that we might be encouraged to a life of consistent prayer.

Deliverance at Cayaman Dyke Ponds
One of those times in my life came on September 6, 1993. Ron and I were vacationing in Jamaica. In one week of birding, I had added forty-one new species to my life list and was feeling elated. That morning, we headed for Cayaman Dyke Ponds to locate the elusive Caribbean coot that my guidebook told me could easily be found in this secluded spot.

Cayaman Dyke Ponds are located on a private sugar plantation. We drove through the plantation until we came to the dike, then walked about a mile along it to where the coots were. Nearby, four men were spearfishing. Curious, Ron stayed a few minutes to talk with them while I headed back toward the car.

Partway back to the car, I heard Ron's voice and turned around to see him handing money to one of the men who had a spear pointed at Ron's throat! Another man stood nearby, spear ready! *Oh, God! What can I do?* I sent a silent prayer to heaven!

"Go to the car, Dorothy!" Ron commanded. "Go quickly!"

I began to run, each step a prayer for Ron's safety and mine. When my side began to hurt, I slowed to a fast walk. I heard steps gaining on me. Then a rough hand snatched at my red shoulder bag, which held my two bird books, pens, and bird list for the trip. I held on until I looked into the man's eyes. There, I saw only evil; I knew he'd use his spear if he wanted to!

"Let him have it!" Ron shouted.

I let go of the bag. The man with the spear ran back toward Ron, and I again started running toward the car. *He's got my bird books!* I felt really upset. *And my list of the trip!*

Again I heard footsteps behind me; this time, they sounded like Ron's. In a moment, he caught up to me and handed over my shoulder bag with the bird books and list still inside.

"As the man passed me, he looked inside and discovered there was no money, only books," Ron said. "He swore and threw the bag back at me!"

We hurried to the car, rejoicing that we were both unharmed; I had my bird books back, and the robber had taken less than fifty dollars. We marveled that he had been blind to the money belt around my waist, which was in full sight! In it were our passports, tickets home, and about $2,000 in traveler's checks.

Angels fight for us

> The vast confederacy of evil is arrayed against all who would overcome; but Christ would have us look to the things which are not seen, to the armies of heaven encamped about all who love God, to deliver them. From what dangers, seen and unseen, we have been preserved through the interposition of the angels, we shall never know, until in the light of eternity we see the providences of God.[7]

In the two weeks leading up to that experience, the Lord had drawn me several times to promises of His protection against evil. "Satan will not yield one inch of ground except as he is driven back by the power of heavenly messengers."[8] "He [God] would sooner send every angel out of heaven to protect His people than leave one soul that trusts in Him to be overcome by Satan."[9]

After reading these promises, I wrote in my journal:

> Wow! Lord, thank You for the possibilities of Your power! You'd do *that* for Dorothy Watts! Please set a hedge about me. Don't let Satan and his angels through to gain the victory in my life! You may have complete control! Thank You for the wonderful victory I have in Your power! Make me more aware of Your presence in all the circumstances of life.

Explore for yourself

1. Think back over your life, beginning as early as you can remember. Make a list of the times you have seen God overcome evil on your behalf. When did God deliver you from temptation or from danger? Then write a prayer of praise and thanksgiving.

2. Study what God is able to do for you: Read Daniel 3:17; Luke 3:8; Acts 20:32; Ephesians 3:20; Philippians 3:21; Hebrews 2:18; Hebrews 7:25; James 4:12; Jude 24. Center your prayer of praise around God's ability to do for you what you cannot do for yourself.

3. Fold a sheet of paper in half. On one side, write the words *I can't!* On the other side, write the words *He can!* For instance: "I can't stop smoking. He can give me the power to overcome the habit!" "I can't love my neighbor after what he did to me. He can give me the victory over my anger and hurt."

4. Begin a program of hiding God's Word in your heart. Choose one promise of Scripture for each week. Write it on several cards, and stick them in conspicuous places where you will see them often to help you fix the text in mind. Place one on your mirror where you can memorize it as you brush your teeth. Place one in your car so that you can read it when you are stuck in traffic. Have one in your billfold so that you can learn it as you wait in a line or for an appointment.

5. Read through the Psalms, underlining each promise of victory in red. When the battle gets rough, turn back to those promises and gather courage.

Explore in a group

1. Did the stories of this chapter bring to mind any incidents in your own life when the Word of God and prayer helped you be victorious over sin and temptation? Share with the group.

2. Try to think of a time when you were delivered from danger by God's intervention. Share with the group.

3. Go around the group, each person offering a sentence prayer of praise for a time when God gave victory in their lives or the lives of someone they know. Go for several rounds, for as long as someone wants to praise God for His marvelous power.

4. This chapter concentrated on only two weapons we can use in our fight against Satan. Read Ephesians 6. Discuss the other methods suggested. Why are these other weapons also important in our battle with sin?

5. Divide into groups of three. Share one area in your life where you need God to give you victory. Pray for each other.

10

Obtaining Healing

*Pray for each other so that you may be healed
(James 4:16, NIV).*

Isobel Kuhn was working as a waitress in Chicago to earn money for tuition at Moody Bible Institute. One hot, humid day she was pouring coffee from a large, steaming tureen when she felt she was going to faint. The room began to spin, and Isobel struggled to stay focused on what she was doing.

I can't faint now! she thought. *Somehow I've got to get this thing turned off! If I don't, boiling coffee will pour over me as I fall!*

"Lord, help me!" she whispered.

Later she wrote, "Instantly a most wonderful thing happened. I felt the Lord Himself come and stand behind my left shoulder. He put His right hand on my right shoulder, and a tingle shot through me from head to foot. Healed completely, I calmly turned off the tureen."

Isobel stood for a moment, praising God for His goodness. Then she turned and picked up her tray. All feelings of nausea and faintness had left her, and she felt a wonderful sense of joy and well-being. The exhilaration of that healing encounter stayed with Isobel for days.[1]

Sometimes God heals immediately

Recently a friend of mine, Rachel Varghese, testified how God had worked quickly, dramatically to heal her. For months, she was in terrible pain but hesitated to go to the doctor because she had no medical coverage. When she finally was forced to go, the doctor told her she had a large tumor, and it would be necessary to operate. Family and friends began to pray earnestly for her. Two friends prayed, "Lord, please heal the tumor so that Rachel won't have to have the operation."

When Rachel went for her sonogram, the doctor was puzzled. "You are in excellent condition!" he exclaimed. "There is no tumor!" It had completely disappeared. There was no need to operate!

Sometimes God works alongside the doctors

I prayed earnestly that the Lord would remove my breast cancer before an operation was necessary. I longed to see a miracle of instant healing so that I could go to the Ukraine with my husband and testify of God's goodness. On the day of my scheduled surgery, I wrote the following prayer:

Lord, how marvelous it would be if there was no cancer there! But however You heal is OK. Just help me to rest in You. I believe healing will come. That's Your job, not mine. You choose the moment and the method.

Early that morning, God led me to read the following passage in *Christ's Object Lessons:*

When trials arise that seem unexplainable, we should not allow our peace to be spoiled. . . . He will shut us in with the bright beams of the Sun of Righteousness. Beyond this Satan cannot penetrate. He cannot pass this shield of holy light.[2]

In response, I prayed:

Thank You, Lord. You are my strength. Help me to feel Your presence by my side. Shut me in with the

bright beams of Your love, and help that love to penetrate to every gene of my body to bring health and
healing. Please be with the technicians and the surgeon
today. Give them wisdom. I go to surgery today trusting
in Your healing power. It's scary, but You will be with
me. Thank You!

Several times before the operation and again later, when I
lay at home recovering, I tried to imagine a sphere of light
surrounding me. It gave me peace to know that God was with
me.

Two months later, the day before my radiation treatments
were to begin, I got a call from the cancer clinic.

"We are not recommending any more treatment," the doctor
said. "We believe you are now all clear."

*Oh, Lord, thank You! Thank You! I won't have to go in for
radiation tomorrow!* I prayed silently.

"This does not mean you are free for life," the doctor warned.
"You are at greater risk now than the average woman. You must
have a checkup and mammogram every six months."

*Gladly, Lord, gladly! Meanwhile, help me know how I can live
a more healthful lifestyle!*

The Lord has answered that prayer. I've changed my diet and
am on a regular exercise program. My weight is coming down.
I feel great! The Lord is so good!

Sometimes God says, "Wait"

For several months, Joyce Landorf had been having pain
following concerts or speaking appointments. The pain became
so intense that it felt as if every tooth was aching, her whole jaw
throbbing, and her head pounding. Nothing she did would
relieve the agony.

About that time, Joyce wrote, "When pain enters your life,
the first practical and logical step is to pray, and so we did. We
prayed for healing and wisdom. I am sure God heard us, but He
decided to usher us into His waiting room."

After four years of enduring pain, visiting all kinds of

specialists, and having no relief, Joyce wrote of her experience in the book *The High Cost of Growing.* In it she shares the lessons God taught her through pain and the precious experience with Him she has discovered in His waiting room.[3]

Martha Nicholson had five major diseases. Eventually she was confined to her bed, unable to move anything but her feet and hands, and she was in perpetual pain. About her experience, she wrote, "Every morning I awake with quick wonder in my heart and wonder what bright new gift He will give me today."[4]

Joni Eareckson Tada, paralyzed from the neck down for nearly thirty years, often reminds herself that Lamentations 3:25 says the Lord is wonderfully good to those who wait for Him. She knows; she's been waiting a long time.[5]

Sometimes God starts by healing our emotions

Negative emotions contribute to the breakdown of health. "Grief, anxiety, discontent, remorse, guilt, distrust, all tend to break down the life forces and to invite decay and death."[6]

When I read that statement, I prayed:

> Lord, forgive me, please! All of these negative emotions have been at work in my life during the past ten years. No wonder I have suffered so much! Lord, heal my thoughts and emotions so that my body might be healed! Take these away from me!

One day I decided it was time to clean my emotional house. I was ready to get rid of some of those negative emotions, and I asked God to bring His wheelbarrow to haul away my garbage!

That day I imagined filling five garbage bags full and giving them to Him to cart away. One bag held resentment, another held jealousy, and still another was full of self-pity. There was a bag full of fear and yet another, with impatience.

As I filled each bag, I tried to remember specific incidents that brought on those feelings. As I thought of each one, I crammed it in the bag and with relief handed over to God all the rotting, stinking mess. How good it felt to be rid of those negative emotions.

Through the months, I filled more garbage bags with guilt, anxiety, and bitterness. I had to get rid of an unforgiving spirit. That was a particularly hard bag to fill. I spent a whole morning's devotion on that one.

> Lord, I really do want to forgive as You have forgiven me, to love others as You love. Here's a list of people in my past who have been hurtful, whom I need to forgive. Lord, please give me a heart of forgiveness and love like Yours. I've thought I'd forgiven these people, but I can still taste the bitterness when they come to mind. Please take all of this away, and give me Your thoughts toward them always!

After that prayer, I listed the names of twenty-four people! I had no idea I'd gathered so much hurt and bitterness. I then wrote, "And, Lord, if there are any others, bring them to mind." Just now, as I reread this list from four years ago, I realized a few more needed to be added! I wrote down six more names, praying that God would give me unconditional love and acceptance for each of them, in spite of how I felt they had hurt me. So the Lord is still working with me, healing not only my body, but also my emotions.

God is always ready to heal us spiritually

Not long ago, I was blessed by the testimony of Annette Stanwick at the British Columbia women's retreat. She shared her miraculous survival after an auto accident that kept her in the hospital for months. At the beginning, she couldn't see because her eyes were swollen shut from her injuries. She couldn't talk either. She knew that she was near death, and she felt unready to die. I wept as she told of how the Lord cradled her in His arms and assured her of His wondrous love and salvation. He took away her fear, filling her heart with a tremendous joy and peace.

She survived and learned to walk again. Looking at her, you would never know what she has been through, except that the glory of the Lord shines from her face as she praises Him for both her physical and spiritual healing.

I, too, can testify that my greatest blessing during encounters with pain and suffering has not been the physical healing, which is marvelous! Instead, it has been the emotional and spiritual healing of His presence!

Explore for yourself

1. Use one or two devotional times for cleaning out the emotional garbage of your mind. What negative emotions do you want the Lord to cart away? List the emotions; then try to think of specific reasons for each emotion. Give the circumstances as well as the feelings to God. He can cleanse and heal your emotions.

2. Read through the book *The Ministry of Healing*. Read a few pages at a time, stopping when the Lord speaks to your heart about a healing process He wants to set in motion in your life. Keep a record of His special messages to you and what you plan to do about each one.

3. Scan *Life Sketches* by Ellen G. White, looking for incidents of healing in answer to prayer. You will be amazed at how much of her early ministry was centered around praying for healing, for herself and for people she met. You will be thrilled as you realize that God is just as willing to hear your prayers for healing as He was for those early Adventists. You may enjoy making a list of the healing stories. Who was healed? What from? How did it happen?

4. Do a study of all the healing incidents in Christ's ministry. Make a devotional study of each story. Read it in several Bible versions. Find the story in *The Desire of Ages*, and compare it with the Bible account. Put yourself into the story as the person who was healed. What insights do you get that will apply to your own life? Find at least one message God has for you in each story.

5. Joni Eareckson Tada writes the letters *PTL* at the bottom

of each painting or drawing she does, all of which have been done with a brush or pen held between her teeth! *PTL* stands for "Praise the Lord." She has learned to give thanks to God in everything, in her helplessness and disability, even though God has not chosen to heal her now. Think of all the bad things that are happening in your life. Begin to consciously thank God for each circumstance.

Share in a group

1. No doubt several in your group have had experiences with healing, either of themselves or someone near to them. Share these stories of God's power.

2. Have you ever been ushered into "God's waiting room," as Joyce Landorf and Joni Eareckson Tada were? How did you react? What did you learn from the experience?

3. We all need healing in some form. Divide into groups of three or four. Share one area where you need healing: physical, emotional, mental, or spiritual. Pray for one another that you may be healed.

4. Assign a different chapter of *The Ministry of Healing* to each person in your group. Have them come back to the next group meeting to share one or two insights they gained in that chapter.

---11---

Gathering Joy

You will fill me with joy in your presence
(Psalm 16:11, NIV).

The edelweiss is a white, star-shaped flower that grows in the mountain regions of Europe, Asia, and South America. Few people have seen this flower, because it grows wild in high regions, where only the hardiest climbers venture. Yet what a joy its soft beauty is to the climber when he or she finds it on some barren crag![1]

In her book *Gold by Moonlight,* Amy Carmichael has an entire chapter about "gathering the edelweiss of God." She likens the flower to the little surprises of joy that can be found in every painful experience.[2]

Amy wrote this book in 1935, four years after she stumbled in the darkness and fell into an open pit, breaking her ankle. Because of complications, Amy was confined to her bed for the next twenty years until her death. Those who knew her reported that her room was always bright with joy and the presence of Christ. She found joy in such things as moonlight on her windowsill, the song of a bird, or the twinkle of stars on a clear night.[3]

Look up, not down

Gail MacDonald writes of a friend who was cheered during a time of pain by her preschooler. The little girl had fallen flat on her back into a mud puddle, and the mother expected a burst of tears.

Instead, the child looked up at the leaves with sudden wonder. "Look! Mommy! See the pretty leaves!"[4]

When you and I fall in the mud, perhaps we need to look up and see the colorful leaves God has provided.

When I read that story, I thought of two lines of a poem I heard many years ago:

Two men looked from the self-same bars;
One saw the mud, the other the stars.

Through the years, I've read a number of biographies about people who spent time in prison. Invariably they found something to rejoice about in the midst of their misery.

The words of Etty Hillesum, written two months before she died in the gas chambers of Auschwitz, illustrate the ability some people have to "gather the edelweiss of God" from the barren wastes of life.

I now realize, God, how much you have given me. So much that was beautiful and so much that was hard to bear. Yet whenever I showed myself ready to bear it, the hard was directly transformed into the beautiful.[5]

Charles Spurgeon once saw a weather vane on a friend's barn that said "God is love."

"What do you mean by that?" Spurgeon asked. "Do you think God is as changeable as the weather?"

"No," his friend replied. "I mean that no matter which way the wind blows, God is still love!"[6]

I, too, have discovered that no matter which way the wind blows in life, God is still love, He is still in control, and He can help me to gather joy in the midst of pain.

Treasures of darkness

During a time of darkness in my life, God gave me the promise of Isaiah 43:3: "I will give thee the treasures of darkness, and hidden riches of secret places, that thou mayest know that I, the Lord, which call thee by thy name, am the God of Israel."

Treasures of darkness—what a beautiful thought, I mused. *In this time of darkness, You have promised to provide a treasure to see me through!* I broke into a smile as I remembered the treasure God had given during another time of darkness.

I thought of the dark hours after my mother's death. During the almost twenty years she had lived with us, she had become more than a mother; she was a dear friend. But suddenly she was gone, and I felt devastated and abandoned.

After crying nonstop for twenty-four hours, I stood at the window of our bedroom in Gresham, Oregon, and gazed at the bleak February landscape. I remember looking up at the gray sky through bare birch branches and crying out, "Oh, God, where are You? I need You here beside me, or I'll never survive. Why are You so far from me? Don't You hear? Don't You even care?"

At that moment, a robin landed on a spruce bough near my window. He cocked his head as though to catch my eye, then sang his heart out.

"What are you doing here?" I asked. And then I knew. He was God's messenger, sent to let me know that heaven had heard! God had sent me a little miracle, the first robin of spring.

I felt something very warm in that moment, as though God had come down to my bedroom and wrapped His arms about me, holding me close. New tears came to my eyes, but this time they were tears of joy and gratefulness for God's presence.

Letting go, letting God

At another time, a cloud of darkness hung over me concerning our children. They were now grown, and all three seemed to be going through times of difficulty. For some reason, I took all of it upon myself; I thought of all the mistakes I had made in mothering them and felt overcome with guilt.

Being highly melancholy in temperament, I gathered up all my failures and disappointments and replayed them. When I ran out of parenting failures, I began to remember all the times

I had not been the perfect wife. Soon I was swinging over the deep chasm of despair.

To show the Lord how awful I felt, I drew Him a picture! I sketched a rugged precipice, a deep chasm, a bare branch sticking out over the cliff, and a rope hanging from the branch with a knot at the end. Then I drew a little stick figure—me—hanging on with both hands.

Beside it I wrote the words "Help! Lord! My strength is almost gone. I can't hold on! I'm scared. Where are You?"

"Go ahead, Dorothy, let go!" He whispered to my frightened heart. "I'm here. I'll catch you." And of course He did. Then He gave me the assurance "Your children are My responsibility, Dorothy. I can make up for your mistakes!"

During the next few days, He brought me several treasures to cherish. One was a call from my son Stephen, who said, "I love you, Mom. I hope you're coming soon. I want to see you!" He sounded upbeat. He'd gotten a job, and things were going better.

Then I got a letter from my daughter Esther that said in part, "It's nice having someone who really knows and understands me, someone with whom I can always be myself. You may not know it, but your support and faith in me have pulled me through more times than I can count. I don't know what I'd do without you in my life!"

I wrote a prayer of gratitude.

Thank You, Lord, for these two affirmations from my children at a time when I've been feeling like a failure. Maybe I didn't do too bad a job after all! Thank You for this joy in the midst of my pain.

Another special aspect was that it was five months after Mother's Day and still two months before my birthday!

Pick flowers, not thorns

Joy is a decision to trust in God and His goodness in spite of the circumstances of life. Joy is a settled confidence that God is in control and that in Him "all will work together for good." Joy sees a rainbow in the rain, a promise of God in each teardrop. Joy is choosing to pick the flowers instead of the thorns along the pathway of life.

Ellen White tells about a woman who wrote to her, dwelling upon the mistakes, failures, and disappointments of her life. That night, Ellen had a dream of a garden.

Ellen was gathering the beautiful flowers, enjoying the lovely fragrance. She was interrupted by crying and turned to see this woman caught in a thicket of briers. "Is it not a pity that this beautiful garden is spoiled with thorns?" she wailed.

The guide, who stood nearby, said, "Let the thorns alone, for they will only wound you. Gather the roses, the lilies, and the pinks."

In reflecting on this dream, Ellen wrote:

> It is not wise to gather together all the unpleasant recollections of a past life,—its iniquities and disappointments,—to talk over them and mourn over them until we are overwhelmed with discouragement.[7]

> Have there not been some bright spots in your experience? Have you not had some precious seasons when your heart throbbed with joy in response to the Spirit of God? When you look back into the chapters of your life experience do you not find some pleasant pages? Are not God's promises, like the fragrant flowers, growing beside your path on every hand? Will you not let their beauty and sweetness fill your heart with joy?[8]

Explore for yourself

1. Go through the garden of your past life. Ignoring the painful times, look rather for the "edelweiss of God," for the "lilies, roses, and pinks" that He has placed there to give you joy. Praise God for each one.

2. Think about a particular dark time in your life during

which God placed "treasures of darkness" for you amidst your trial and pain. Try to enumerate those treasures.

3. In her book *Loneliness*, Elisabeth Elliot shares a process she uses to offer her loneliness to God.[9] Try it with loneliness or some other unwanted pain. Here are her steps:

a. Kneel with open hands before the Lord. Be silent and become aware of His presence.

b. Visualize the unwanted pain as one of God's gifts to you. He has placed it in your hands for a reason.

c. Try to think of something about the gift for which you can truly thank Him. If nothing else, thank Him for His sovereign will that allowed you to have such a gift.

d. Thank Him for His unfailing love, the promise of His presence, and the good He is working out of your pain.

e. Then offer up your unwanted gift to God, and with it your love, acceptance, thanksgiving, and trust that He will use it for His glory and your good.

4. Read Isaiah 43 in several versions, if possible.

In it are at least seven reasons why we should find joy and confidence in the Lord in spite of our trials and difficulties. Can you find them all?

5. Give yourself a gift of solitude with God. Ask Him to give you joy. Take a long, warm bath with soft music and bubble bath. Curl up on the couch with a cup of hot tea and the Psalms. Go to the zoo and let yourself laugh. Lie in the backyard and look at the stars.

Share in a group

1. Think about some of the "treasures of darkness" you have experienced in life. Allow a quiet time of silent meditation; then share with the group what you have remembered.

2. Assign one of the following texts to each person: Psalm 43:4; Nehemiah 8:10; Psalm 48:2; Psalm 30:5; Psalm 126:5; Psalm 16:11; Ecclesiastes 2:26; Isaiah 55:11, 12; Zephaniah 3:17; Psalm 51:8, 12; Psalm 27:6; Luke 15:7; John 16:24; Galatians 5:22; Hebrews 12:2; James 1:2, 3. Allow five or ten minutes of quiet time to meditate on the verse. Then have each

person share what that verse speaks to him or her about joy.

3. Have your meeting around a campfire or a fireplace. Sit around the fire, sing favorite songs, and reminisce about times God has brought joy into your lives.

4. Place a gift-wrapped box in the center of the group. Ask each person to think of "unwanted gifts" that God has allowed him or her to have, such as loneliness, sickness, disability, unemployment, a dysfunctional family, problems at work, or whatever. Write these "unwanted gifts" on slips of paper. Invite the members to offer their "unwanted gift" back to God along with their acceptance, love, and thanksgiving for that very gift, asking Him to use it for His glory and their good.

5. Read Isaiah 43 through together. Try to find seven reasons why we should be joyful in times of difficulty. Make a list of these reasons on a chart or whiteboard.

12

Seeking Peace

*You will keep in perfect peace him whose mind is
steadfast, because he trusts in you (Isaiah 26:3, NIV).*

C anon Gibbon, vicar of Harrogate, England, spoke on this
verse one Sunday in August 1875.

> The original Hebrew version of this text reads "sha-
> lom, shalom," the vicar said. We could translate it,
> "Thou wilt keep him in peace peace whose mind is
> stayed on Thee." Thus by repeating the word, the
> Hebrew conveys the meaning of absolute perfection, or
> perfect peace.

Edward Bickersteth happened to be in the audience that
summer day. The phrases *peace, peace* and *perfect peace* stuck
in Edward's mind. That very afternoon, Edward visited a dying
relative in Liverpool who was greatly depressed.

Casting about for words of encouragement, Edward thought
of the morning's sermon. He opened his Bible and read, "I will
keep him in perfect peace whose mind is stayed on thee."

"That's a promise for you," Edward said. "Look to Jesus. Take
your eyes off your circumstances, and look to the Saviour. He
has promised you perfect peace. Peace can be yours in all the
sorrows, troubles, and uncertainties of life."

Going to a nearby desk, Edward found a piece of paper and
quickly wrote the words of the hymn "Peace, Perfect Peace."[1] He

then read the poem to his dying relative, just as it appears in the hymnal.[2]

What is peace?

Peace is a treasure we find in prayer. Like a sparkling diamond, its facets reflect God's power. Peace is so complex that it touches every aspect of our lives, bringing calmness, wholeness, rightness, and a sense of well-being.

To understand what peace is, we need to look first at what it is not. Some antonyms of the word *peace* are *war, rebellion, hostility, chaos, turmoil, discord, conflict, alienation, division, dissension,* and *disunity.*

Peace in the political arena means the cessation of combat, the signing of a treaty. In the world of weather, peace suggests the absence of wind, thunder, lightning, and the fury of the elements. Peace in a relationship means the end of alienation and is symbolized by a kiss or handshake. For our emotional world, peace means the end to turmoil, conflict, anxiety, worry, and frustration. In the spiritual realm, peace is the end of our rebellion against God; it is achieved by coming around to God's viewpoint and being willing to trust Him.

No peace without surrender

No matter in which sphere of life we want peace, we cannot have peace without surrender. Something must always be given up in exchange for peace. Countries choose to give up demands, territory, or arms. People often yield their opinions, rights, pride, and selfishness in order to be friends.

If we would have peace with God, we must come to the place of submitting everything we have and are to Jesus Christ. This includes our hearts, bodies, minds, feelings, talents, gifts, personalities, dreams, work, friends, families, possessions, and wills. Elisabeth Elliot calls this "the glad surrender."[3] She says that when we truly yield all we are to God, then God brings us "through the world's fog to His island of peace."[4]

The day I discovered the message of Isaiah 26:3, I wrote in my journal:

Lord, I hear You saying, "Dorothy, if you are not at peace with Me, the problem is not Mine; it's yours! I know what is best. Get to know Me. Agree with Me. Stop fighting. Submit to Me. When you do, you will be at peace."

Lord, this is my desire. Remind me that in my choleric temperament, all too often I think my way is the only way. I need to be more ready to see Your side, and even when I can't understand, to just accept it and submit to Your will.

Submission means peace. Peace means lack of conflict. Lack of conflict is lack of stress. Lack of stress is lack of disease. Lack of disease is health. Health is joy and a sense of fulfillment and well-being, wholeness, and rightness in life. And it all begins with surrender!

As I copied the words of "Peace, Perfect Peace" into my journal, I noticed that the poem addresses five difficult situations in which we can discover perfect peace: (1) the dark world of sin, (2) the pressing duties of life, (3) sorrow and disappointment, (4) concern for loved ones far away, and (5) the unknown future.

"In this dark world of sin"

Twelve-year-old Ellen Harmon feared that she could never become worthy to be called a child of God. She wrote:

I had often sought for the peace there is in Christ, but I could not seem to find the freedom I desired. A terrible sadness rested on my heart. I could not think of anything I had done to cause me to feel sad; but it seemed to me that I just was not good enough to enter heaven, that such a thing would be altogether too much for me to expect.[5]

The summer of 1840 Ellen went to a camp meeting in Buxton, Maine, with her family. Determined to find pardon and peace, she knelt in the sawdust after a service and prayed, "Help, Jesus; save me, or I perish!"

She said, "Suddenly my burden left me, and my heart felt light."

An older woman came to where she knelt. She put her arm around Ellen and asked, "Dear child, have you found Jesus?"

Surprised, Ellen looked up at her. She was just about to say, "Yes," when the woman interrupted her.

"Indeed you have; His peace is with you, I can see it in your face!"[6]

During a week-long seminar I was giving, I had a similar experience. Satan came to me with a list of my mistakes, failures, and sins of the past. I clung to the promise of 1 John 1:9: "If we confess our sins, he is faithful and just to forgive us our sins and to cleanse us from all unrighteousness."

In the quietness, I heard the Lord say:

Dorothy, I want to take away your guilt. I offer you peace. I died for your sins. I died to give you peace and power! In Me it is as though you had never sinned. Trust Me, Dorothy. Accept My gift of peace.

Peace came as I surrendered everything to Him, leaning back into His arms of love, resting in His promise.

"By thronging duties pressed"

I sat on the beach at Deer Lake Park early one morning. It was an island of peace and quiet in the midst of busy, bustling Burnaby, British Columbia. Distant skyscrapers and nearby palatial homes were mirrored in the still lake.

That scene was the very opposite of how I felt inside. As I expressed it to the Lord that morning, "I feel AWFUL." Then, taking the letters of the word *awful,* I made an acrostic of my feelings and offered them to the Lord. I felt **A**nxious about the new school year, **W**orried about how I'd get everything done, **F**rustrated with circumstances, **U**pset about something that had happened, and **L**oaded down with work. After laying out each feeling before the Lord in detail, I prayed: "Dear Father, this is how I feel. I'm but a little child coming to You in tears of frustration, seeking Your peace, Your love, Your comfort, and Your strength."

For a long while I sat there in the stillness, letting a sense of God's presence wash over me. I listened as He spoke words of assurance, comfort, and hope. At last, I was able to write: "Thank You, Father! I love You! I no longer feel awful. I feel GREAT! **G**ood, **R**elaxed, **E**nergetic, **A**ble, and **T**hankful!"

"With sorrows surging round"

At one time of great disappointment and sorrow in my life, the Lord brought His peace through the following words of hope:

Above the distractions of the earth He sits enthroned; all things are open to His divine survey; and from His great and calm eternity He orders that which His providence sees best.[7]

All the perplexities of life's experience will then be made plain. Where to us have appeared only confusion and disappointment, broken purposes and thwarted plans, will be seen a grand, overruling, victorious purpose, a divine harmony.[8]

I wrote that day in my journal:

I love that phrase *calm eternity*. This moment in time, now, seems so confusing and tumultuous. If only I could view it, not from my perspective in the center of the storm, but from the calmness of God's eternal perspective, how different I would feel!

That evening, still feeling the pain of my situation, I sat at the piano and began to play through the hymnal. At first, I banged out my frustration loudly, but gradually the message of the songs began to get through to me, messages of peace and

God's control. My playing grew gentler, calmer. At last, I picked up my journal and wrote:

> Lord, please help me to remember that above and through all, You are working out Your will for my life, that You are in control. Nothing comes my way without Your permission. Thank You for the peace this thought gives!

"With loved ones far away"

I felt so helpless the morning of November 22, 1993. My brother lay in critical condition nearly three thousand miles away in Dayton, Ohio. His wife, Pat, had phoned, weeping out the news. Don had aneurysms in the artery leading to the stomach. He had kidney stones. Then they discovered a heart problem that demanded surgery.

"I wish you could be here with Don," Pat said.

I wished I could too, but for a number of reasons, it was not possible. In my concern for my brother so far away, I prayed a Palms Down, Palms Up prayer, casting all of my cares at the feet of Jesus.

> Lord, I've got a lot to give You this morning. My need for You is so great! Here's what I need You to take: (1) my concern about Donald; (2) Don's many problems; (3) Pat's helplessness and loneliness in this crisis.
>
> Now, Lord, I'm waiting on You with my hands open, ready to receive what only You can give: (1) Your healing presence to be with my brother; (2) Your strength uplifting Pat; (3) Your gift of peace for myself.

My pulse rate slowed as His peace settled over me. I put into words His soothing message to me:

> Dorothy, I am near, so very near to You. Right now, I am by Don's bed; My hand is on his shoulder. My power is flowing through him to accomplish My will. So do not be anxious about anything!

I was comforted all day by the image of Christ's presence by Don's bedside, His left hand on Don's right shoulder. It continued to cheer me during the next five months as Don went through quadruple bypass surgery and a second surgery to repair six aneurysms. What a wonderful God! What a terrific friend!

"Our future all unknown"

One of the stresses of being married to a conference worker is the news that your husband's name is on a list for a position that would mean a move for the family. In the thirty-five years Ron and I have been married, his name has been on a list for departmental or administrative positions at least thirty times.

Most times have meant a period of several days or even weeks before a decision was voted. During the years I was a teacher, it seemed to be by some diabolical design that these lists happened just when I needed to be signing a teaching contract for the next year or when I had just signed one! Fortunately, in only a few instances did we actually receive a call; but always the time of not knowing was difficult.

During one such time, God's message to me was John 14:27: "My peace I give unto you." I wrote an ACTS prayer in response:

> **A - Adoration.** Lord, I praise You this morning for who You are, the almighty God of the universe. You are the One who controls the elements, the nations, and Your church.
>
> **C - Confession.** I confess how often I let my heart be troubled and afraid because of conditions in the world, the deliberations of committees, and the circumstances of daily life that I can't control.
>
> **T - Thanksgiving.** But, Lord, I thank You that You are in control. Your hand is over the nations, over Your church, and over our lives. I am thankful my future is in Your hands!
>
> **S - Supplication.** Today, I ask You for Your peace. I need it today that I might rest in You no matter what happens. When my heart is starting to be troubled, when I am tempted to fret, speak to me of Your peace.

Explore for yourself

1. Write an ACTS prayer about an area of your life that is in turmoil. Submit it to Him, and be at peace.

2. Find "Peace, Perfect Peace" in a hymnal. Read or sing the words, and think how they speak to the experience of your own life.

Try to think of a time that God spoke to you in each of these five typical difficult situations.

3. What do the following texts tell you about the conditions for peace? Psalm 4:8; 29:11; 34:14; 119:165; Luke 8:48; John 14:27; Romans 14:17, 19; Galatians 5:22; Ephesians 2:14; 2 Thessalonians 3:16.

4. What areas of your life seem to be out of control? Sketch a gift package. Underneath the gift, write all the parts of your life that you are willing to give back to God for Him to take complete control of. Give Him complete freedom to do whatever He likes with your gifts. Rest in the knowledge that He never makes a mistake.

5. When you are feeling a sense of unrest and a lack of peace, make as precise a list as possible of your feelings: annoyance, anger, frustration, aggravation, anxiety, worry, concern, upset, burdened, cornered, hopeless, helpless, etc. Write a few sentences explaining the situation that brought on a particular feeling. Then give the situation and the feeling to God, asking Him to exchange it for peace and the knowledge that He is in control.

6. Write a Palms Down, Palms Up prayer based on your concerns.

7. An artist once painted a picture of a bird sitting quietly on her nest in the middle of a raging storm. He titled it "Peace."

Draw your own sketch of peace.

Explore in a group

1. Sing "Peace, Perfect Peace" together. Pause after each verse, and let members share about times in their lives when God spoke "Peace" to them in such a situation.

2. What is the one thing that is causing you most concern at

the present time? Share it with the members of your group. Pray for one another by name and the situation mentioned. Ask God to take control, bringing peace.

3. Discuss the statement "There is no peace without surrender." Do you agree or disagree with the author? Give your own examples of what has to be given up in various situations for peace to occur.

4. Brainstorm to make a list of things we give up to become followers of Christ. What does He give in exchange? List these things in parallel columns on a chart or chalkboard.

5. Put on some quiet music. Meditate on peace. What pictures of peace come to mind? What are the sounds of peace? What is the touch of peace like? Turn off the music, and share peace images.

PART THREE

Exploring Intercessory Prayer

13

Discovering Power

*The prayer of a righteous man is powerful
and effective (James 5:16, NIV).*

It was nearly seven o'clock on Christmas Eve in Seattle. A
cold rain had begun to fall as Jack Bryan shuffled along
the sidewalk, his head down.

I'm a failure, he thought. *My business went broke. The bank
has repossessed our car. There's no money for food or rent. I can't
get a job. How can I go home empty-handed on Christmas Eve?*

Distraught, Jack walked to a deserted park. He closed his
eyes, pointed a revolver to his head, and was about to pull the
trigger, when a mighty blow knocked the gun from his hand.
Jack opened his eyes to see a stranger standing before him.

At seven o'clock, Alexander Lake, a police reporter for a
Seattle newspaper, had been sitting at his typewriter in the
newsroom three blocks away when an unexplained impulse
caused him to run to the park just in time to save Jack's life.

"Let's go talk about this over a bowl of hot soup," Alex
suggested to the trembling man.

At the restaurant, Alex called to tell his editor where he was.
The editor ordered him to the site of a suspected murder. Not
wanting to leave Jack alone, Alex took him along.

Jack followed Alex to the small, ramshackle house where the
dead woman lay on a broken-down bed. At the foot stood her
husband and five small children sobbing softly.

The sight was too much for Jack. "Take me home," he whispered to Alex. "I must have been crazy. I didn't know what misery was. I'd forgotten how much I love them. Take me home."

When they reached Jack's cottage, he ran ahead of the reporter, threw open the kitchen door, and grabbed his wife. He stood there with his eyes closed, holding her as if he'd never let her go. A small girl hugged each of his legs.

Alex heard Jack's wife say, "When you didn't come home by seven o'clock, I knelt and asked God to take care of you and bring you home safely. Now, here you are!"

Suddenly Alex knew why he'd felt the impulse to go out into that cold, wet night at exactly seven o'clock. He had experienced the direct results of intercessory prayer.[1]

What is intercessory prayer?

Dick Eastman defines intercession as "love on its knees."[2] Richard Foster agrees: "If we truly love people, we will desire for them far more than it is within our power to give them, and this will lead us to prayer. Intercession is a way of loving others."[3]

E. M. Bounds defines intercession as simply "talking to God for men."[4] It is asking on behalf of someone else.

According to Wesley L. Duewel, intercessory prayer is part of our duty as Christians. It is exercising our right to go before the mercy seat of the heavenly sanctuary on behalf of others. Intercession is part of our privilege in the priesthood of all believers. It is the awesome opportunity to be a prayer partner with Jesus Christ, mediating for others before God's throne.[5]

"We stand at God's side, working together with Him, in the task of redeeming others," says Edward Bauman.[6]

"Nothing is more important than Intercessory Prayer," declares Richard J. Foster. "People today desperately need the help that we can give them. Marriages are being shattered. Children are being destroyed. Individuals are living lives of quiet desperation, without purpose or future. And we can make a difference . . . if we will learn to pray on their behalf."[7]

The power of intercessory prayer

Morris Venden tells of a series of prayer meetings at a church he pastored. Wondering whether intercession really made a difference in people's lives, the members decided to experiment. They would choose an "impossible case," pray for that case in prayer meeting and at home, and wait to see the results.

Pastor Venden suggested a family he had visited that very day. They had once been members of the church but had become bitter, disillusioned, and angry. As Pastor Venden had left the house, they said, "Don't even pray for us!"

The members agreed they would concentrate their intercessory prayer on that family. That week, the family's house burned down. The second week, a valuable piece of equipment was stolen.

On the last Sabbath of the month, the entire family walked into church! After church, several members told the pastor, "We ought to do more praying!"[8]

I remember putting Susan on my prayer list. She had been a member of my youth Sabbath School class but no longer came to church. I visited her regularly and prayed for her daily.

After several months of earnest intercession with no results, I was asked to offer the opening prayer in Sabbath School, and I felt impressed to pray publicly for Susan.

In prayer I claimed the promises of 1 John 5:14-16. I said, "Lord, I claim these promises for Susan. Put within her a desire to come back to You. Help her just now to want to be here."

When I got up from my knees, I saw Susan just walking in the door of the church! My heart was filled with joy as I went to greet her! The last I knew, Susan was still attending church faithfully. How glad I am that I interceded for her!

Why does intercessory prayer work? I don't understand it fully, but evidently God is bound by certain limitations. Because He has given everyone freedom to choose whom he or she will serve, God will never force entrance into a person's heart. Although He is anxious to work on a person's behalf, He will not do it until he or she asks, or until someone else appeals the case to Him. Our prayers free God to work in a way that would otherwise not be possible.[9]

Dr. E. Stanley Jones put it this way:

In prayer you align yourselves to the purpose and power of God and He is able to do things through you that He couldn't do otherwise. This is an open universe, where some things are left open, contingent upon our doing them. If we do not do them, they will never be done. For God has left certain things open to prayer—things which will never be done except as we pray.[10]

Dick Eastman notes that "when we talk with God in eternity we will quickly learn everything of worth that was accomplished was connected to an intercessor's prayer."[11]

Four rules for intercessory prayer

1. Be specific. Most of our prayers are so general that we don't know whether or not they are answered. How often we offer clichés to God in the place of real intercession: "Bless the sick and afflicted, the missionaries and the colporteurs, our church leaders and our youth."

A bedridden woman in Springfield, Illinois, sick for seventeen years, had been praying in a general way for people in her town to accept Christ. When she finally understood that she must be specific, she wrote down the names of fifty-seven people. She prayed for them three times a day. By and by, she saw all fifty-seven accept Jesus as their personal Saviour.[12]

I well remember my first specific intercessory prayer list. To my amazement, I had visible answers to every one of those thirty-three requests within six months. During those six months, I saw more definite answers to prayer than I had seen in the previous thirty years!

2. Be persistent. Elizabeth had an unconverted husband whom she was anxious to have accept Jesus as his personal Saviour. However, her husband had forbidden her to even mention God in his presence.

She said to herself, "I am going to pray for his conversion every day for twelve months." Every day, she kept her promise, pleading on her knees for the salvation of her husband. At the end of the year, there was no difference.

"I suppose, God, I could keep up six more months," she prayed. "Won't You please work a miracle in his life?"

After six months, there was still no change, so she told the Lord, "I will pray for him as long as You give me breath."

That very evening, her husband came home and without a word went to his room. The meal on the table was getting cold, and still he hadn't come. Worried, she went to see what was wrong.

Elizabeth found him on his knees, pleading with God for mercy. He became a strong member of the church and a powerful witness to the power of intercessory prayer.[13]

Augustine is another example of the power of intercession. His mother, Monica, prayed for his conversion from the moment of his birth. However, when he was a teenager, Augustine ran away from home and succumbed to the temptations of the world.

His wayward life nearly broke Monica's heart, but she would not give up praying for him. One day, tears streaming down her face, she talked to a Christian teacher about her son.

"Go thy way," the teacher said. "God will help thee. It is not possible that the child of these tears should perish."

God answered Monica's prayers in a remarkable way. By chance, Augustine went to Milan and met Ambrose, a godly man. Augustine shared with him the emptiness and restlessness of his heart. He told of the wicked things he'd done and the places he had gone, but nowhere was he able to escape the memory of his mother's prayers.

As a result of that new friendship, Augustine gave his heart to God, and Monica attended the baptism. What a joyous day! Augustine became a famous Christian author of the fourth century. Once he wrote, "It was owing to the faithful and daily prayers of my mother that I did not perish."[14]

My own mother prayed for my brother Donald until the day of her death, but he still had not yielded his life to God. Not long after her funeral, he came back to God and the church. What joy will be hers on the resurrection morning!

3. Be courteous. Intercessory prayer is often discouraging, because the individual we are praying for may have no interest in our prayers. We are dealing here with a mix of divine influence and human choice. God will never compel; He always invites. He respects each person's freedom of choice, his or her right to reject divine love. God will woo but never insist. We must be careful in our relationship with those on our prayer list to have the courtesy of Jesus. We must never use prayer as a type of manipulation to get them to do what we want; rather, we must allow them complete freedom.

4. Be patient. In this day of fast food and fax machines, we are conditioned to expect instant solutions in answer to our prayers of intercession.

John Calvin had the right idea. He once wrote, "We must repeat the same supplications not twice or three times only, but as often as we have need, a hundred and a thousand times. We must never be weary in waiting for God's help."[15]

At several women's retreats, I have introduced the idea of "eggs prayers." The idea is to write out a prayer of intercession and then hide it away in a safe place, waiting for God to hatch it out in His own time. Over the last two years, I have collected many prayers in my "eggs basket" that I present to the Lord daily, asking Him to intercede on behalf of these people.

I have a file folder of letters I've received from women who have written about how their "eggs" have begun to hatch! It's exciting! One tells about the resolution of a difficult problem at work, another of a job for her husband, and yet another of a husband who has begun to soften toward religion. I'm hearing stories of children coming back to God, a return of warmth to churches, and God's healing power at work. God is so good! But sometimes we just need to be patient and let Him work!

Ask Harold

Five-year-old Billy sat listening to his mom and dad discuss a perplexing problem.

"Whatever are we going to do?" sighed Mother.

"I don't know." Father shook his head, worry lines wrinkling his forehead. "I can't think of anyone else I could go to for help.

There doesn't seem to be any help for us."

"Why don't you ask Harold to help?" Billy asked.

"Harold?" Father was puzzled. "Who's Harold? I don't know any Harold. Do you, Mother?"

Mother shook her head.

"Yes, you do!" Billy insisted. "You know, 'Our Father which art in heaven, Harold be thy name!' "

How often I have been like Billy's mom and dad, worrying, fretting, and stewing about people and situations that need changing. I try everything I know to do, and nothing works. Why do I not just turn to the One who can make a real difference? Why don't I spend more time interceding on their behalf? Why isn't my prayer list longer?

Explore for yourself

1. Keep a written list of people for whom you want to pray regularly. Pray through the list, visualizing each person, mentioning his or her name to the Lord and any concerns you have.

2. Keep a promise list. Beside each name, write a Bible promise you are claiming for that particular person.

3. Make up a photo album of missionaries, friends, and family for whom you want to pray regularly. Work through the album each week, praying for the people in the pictures.

4. Draw a set of six concentric circles. Beginning with the smallest, inner circle, write the word *family.* Then on each successive circle moving outward, write the following words in order: *friends, enemies, church leaders, community leaders,* and *world leaders.* In this prayer you are reaching ever outward to a larger group of people. You may want to concentrate on one circle of prayer for each day of the week.

5. You may want to use Nancy Van Pelt's *Prayer Notebook.*[16] It contains six dividers: Monday, Tuesday, Wednesday, Thursday, Friday, Saturday/Sunday. She suggests dividing your intercessory prayer to address one area of concern each day. Each person could make his or her own list of areas. Nancy's list includes: Monday (personal), Tuesday (husband), Wednesday (family), Thursday (friends), Friday (church and community),

Saturday/Sunday (prayer requests noted at church).

6. Make your Christmas-card list your prayer list. Some people keep their Christmas cards and letters in a basket beside their place of prayer. Each day they take out one of the cards and pray for that person and their family as the focus of their intercessory prayer. The card may then be discarded or moved to the bottom of the pile to be prayed for again as it comes up.

Explore in a group

1. This idea comes from Ruthie Jacobson, who got it from the Littauers. Ruthie explained how she used it with a small prayer group. Each member chose a text that would be his or her text for the year. Each day the members prayed for each other through their chosen Bible verse, asking the Lord to do for that person just as He had promised to do.[17]

2. Have a group prayer journal. Each week, members write in requests. They also make note of answered prayers from previous weeks. The entire group prays for all the requests in the journal.

3. Make an intercessory prayer chain. Write out requests on cut strips of colored paper. Join these together to make a prayer chain. Add names and requests from week to week.

4. Cut out some paper eggs. Let members write out their "eggs prayers" on the eggs. Put them in a special basket. Each week bring out the basket, place it in the prayer circle, and pray for the unhatched eggs.[18]

—————14—————

Facilitating Change

Love each other as I have loved you
(John 15:12, NIV).

G rant Swank sat on the edge of the bed and looked down at his son, Jay. The boy was curled up under the blankets, his face turned toward the wall.

He's expecting another scolding, Grant thought. *Should I bring up his wrongdoing now in prayer, lecturing him in the presence of the Lord? Or should I be more concerned with healing his hurt and restoring our relationship?*

Just then, Jay turned his face on the pillow, looking up at Grant with liquid brown eyes. Dad's own heart melted as he realized how very much he loved his son. Grant bowed his head and began:

> Dear Lord, Thank You for Jay. You know how much I love him. He means the world to me. Thank You for giving him to us. May he always serve You. Now we ask You for a good night's sleep. Be near us all, and help tomorrow to be a good day. In Jesus' name, amen.

Jay reached up and hugged his dad tightly. Grant folded his arms around his son.

"Daddy, do you love me even when I'm bad?" Jay whispered.

"Yes," Grant replied, giving him a squeeze, "I always love you."

"You're the best daddy in the world," Jay said, laying his head on Grant's shoulder.[1]

Thank You, Lord, for this moment, Grant thought. *Thank You for helping me to remember that love overlooks wrongs.*

That night, Grant Swank loved Jay as God had loved him. Without realizing it, Grant followed Christ's model for facilitating change. It is as simple as ABC.

A - **Accept.** Grant accepted Jay just as he was, a child who had made mistakes, but one who also had marvelous possibilities for growth. He didn't scold or lecture. He didn't shame or blame. He simply loved. He was more concerned about healing the hurt and restoring the relationship than he was in pointing out error.

B - **Believe.** Grant believed in the infinite possibilities for growth in Jay. He believed that if he gave him freedom, Jay would want to do better. Grant chose to believe in the positive aspects of Jay's character and that if Jay were given the chance, he would have the desire for change.

C - **Commit.** Grant prayed for Jay. He committed him into the hands of the only One who can ever make change happen. He gave Jay into the care of the only One who had the power to help Jay overcome his tendencies to wrongdoing. Instead of using prayer as a form of subtle manipulation, Grant simply prayed for Jay.

Let's take a closer look of Christ's model for facilitating change.

Accept

In Christ's ministry we can see many examples of this total, unconditional acceptance of sinners—in contrast to the more natural, human way of dealing with error.

Levi-Matthew, a publican, was "despised as an apostate, and was classed with the vilest of society"[2] by most people. Yet Jesus called him to be one of His disciples. He accepted an invitation to a banquet in Matthew's home and was just as open and accepting of all the other tax collectors gathered there. Against the religious, social, and national customs of the day, Jesus accepted Levi-Matthew unconditionally.

Zacchaeus, another tax collector, had heard of this teacher who accepted publicans and went out of his way to see such a man. How thrilled he was when Jesus noticed him. Jesus showed His total acceptance of Zacchaeus by going to his house to eat with him.

As a result of Jesus' acceptance of the publicans, they

> longed to become worthy of His confidence. Upon their thirsty hearts His words fell with blessed, life-giving power. New impulses were awakened, and the possibility of a new life opened to these outcasts of society.[3]

The Lord did not condemn the woman caught in adultery. To her, He said, "Neither do I condemn thee." His acceptance awakened in her the desire to be different.

To the woman at the well, a Samaritan and shunned by Jews, Jesus showed His acceptance by asking for a drink of water and by offering her the blessings of heaven. Even when Jesus convinced her that He had "read the secrets of her life; yet she felt that He was her friend, pitying and loving her. While the very purity of His presence condemned her sin, He had spoken no word of denunciation, but had told her of His grace."[4]

How often, through a rehearsal of misdeeds, we cut even deeper the wounds of someone who has sinned, instead of seeking for a way to bring hope and healing.

> Love's agencies have wonderful power, for they are divine. The soft answer that "turneth away wrath," the love that "suffereth long, and is kind," the charity that "covereth a multitude of sins". . . would we learn the lesson, with what power for healing would our lives be gifted! How life would be transformed, and the earth become a very likeness and foretaste of heaven![5]

Forgive me, Lord, for the times I have been more ready to point out error than I have been to offer the healing, restoring power of acceptance.

Believe

Christ looked upon people, saw both the good and the bad traits of character, but chose to believe that the individual—if given a chance—would want to develop the good. He believed in the power of choice that He had placed within each person. He believed in their infinite possibilities for growth and development. He chose to express trust and confidence, rather than disappointment and doubt.

The trust Jesus showed in asking the Samaritan woman for a drink awakened trust within her. By sharing some of the most profound truths of salvation with this immoral woman, Jesus showed His belief in what she could become, by His power—a wonderful witness of His love. She did not disappoint Him.[6]

> He taught all to look upon themselves as endowed with precious talents, which if rightly employed would secure for them eternal riches. . . . He passed by no human being as worthless, but sought to apply the saving remedy to every soul.[7]

So powerful was His affirmation of the possibilities in each human being that His belief in them gave the strength needed to believe in themselves.

In the case of Mary Magdalene, who had been looked upon as a great sinner,

> Christ knew the circumstances that had shaped her life. He might have extinguished every spark of hope in her soul, but He did not. . . . When to human eyes her case appeared hopeless, Christ saw in Mary capabilities for good. He saw the better traits of her character. The plan of redemption has invested humanity with great possibilities, and in Mary these possibilities were to be realized.[8]

Christ believed in Mary when no one else believed in her, when she hadn't even the faith to believe in herself. He saw in her not a failure, but a possibility for His power to work.

Forgive me, Lord, for focusing so much on the flaws in other people, rather than looking at the good points of their characters. Help me to catch a glimpse of the infinite possibilities in each one for whom I intercede. Help me to believe in them as You do.

Commit

The disciples seemed so slow to change—in spite of Christ's demonstrations of unconditional love, in spite of His expressions of belief in them! He understood that without the power of God to do the work, they never could change. So He prayed for them.

> The Saviour knew the character of the men whom He had chosen; all their weaknesses and errors were open before Him; . . . and His heart yearned over these chosen ones. Alone upon a mountain near the Sea of Galilee He spent the entire night in prayer for them.[9]

During the night of Christ's trial, when Peter denied his Lord, the knowledge that Christ had prayed for him gave Peter hope. He remembered how Jesus had said, "I'm praying for you that your faith does not falter. After you survive the test and come back to Me, you'll be able to inspire your brothers in the faith."

Jesus did more than accept Mary Magdalene; He did more than express belief in her. He also prayed for her.

> Seven times she had heard His rebuke of the demons that controlled her heart and mind. She had heard His strong cries to the Father in her behalf. She knew how offensive is sin to His unsullied purity, and in His strength she had overcome.[10]

Jesus did more than accept the Samaritan woman. He did

more than express His belief in her. He also prayed for her. Now, it doesn't say that in the biblical narrative. However, I noticed it while reading the story in *The Desire of Ages*.

When the disciples came back, they found "Him silent, absorbed, as in rapt meditation. His face was beaming with light, and they feared to interrupt His communion with heaven."[11] I feel certain He was praying for that woman as she went back to the village to witness of her encounter.

Help me, Lord, to follow Your example, to commit into the Father's hands all of those on my prayer list who need to change. I don't know all the circumstances of their lives, but You do. You know how best to bring about change. Help me, Lord, not to try to do Your work, but to allow Your Holy Spirit to do the job!

As I have loved you

How does God love us? Is there anything we can do that will cause Him to love us less? Is there anywhere we can go to escape His matchless love? Does He not still love us, even when He sees that discipline is necessary? Is there anything we can do that He will not forgive? When we repent, does He not always in His mercy accept us again as though we had never sinned?

In the same way, we are to love one another. That's the kind of love Jose Manuel Quishpe Pilamunga of San Bernardo, Ecuador, experienced.

The problem started when he went to bed with a woman who was not his wife. He was a deacon and knew better. He knew he had sinned, for the commandment clearly says, "Thou shalt not commit adultery." Soon the whole community knew what had happened.

The pastor and elders visited him and explained the necessity of church discipline. They took away his office, and his name was dropped from membership.

"We love you, and we are sorry we have to do this," the pastor told him. "We want you to repent of your sin, come back to the Lord, and back to the church. We will be praying for you and will welcome your return."

"I resented that very much," Jose says now. "Looking back,

I now realize that even though their response was severe, it was done out of love. All that time when I felt so resentful, they were praying for me, hoping that I would come back to the Lord."

After a year of struggle, Jose returned to the Lord, confessed his sin, and asked forgiveness, first of his wife, then of the church community. He was welcomed back with open arms. A year later he was made the church treasurer and after a few years the president of the community council.

"It is just like that incident is buried," Jose says. "When I pray it seems as though it never happened. My wife and daughters don't say, 'Look what you did.' I am accepted by my God, my family, and my church as though I had never sinned."[12]

Jose now has a deeper understanding of the unconditional love of God because of the way his family and church treated him.

I pray, Lord, that if Jose came back to my church, I would have enough of Your love to accept him. Is there someone I know whom You have already forgiven whom I also need to forgive? Help me to follow Your model for facilitating change in those I love.

Explore for yourself

1. Think about one person you love who needs to change. Write his or her name on a piece of paper. List all of the good traits of character on one side and all of their bad traits of character that need changing on the other side. Tear off the side with the things that need changing, offer them to God asking Him to do the work however He sees fit, then throw the paper away—signifying your desire to leave all of that to God. Spend time praising God for all of the good traits of character you have listed.

2. Find a way as soon as possible to affirm one of the good traits of character you see in the person you are praying for. Each time you see the person, give some word of affirmation. Ask God to help you really accept the person as he or she is, a total package, of good and bad.

3. Every time you are tempted to lecture people about how

they should be different from the way they are, breathe a silent prayer, asking God to help you keep quiet and let Him do His work. Instead of pointing out their errors, send up silent prayers on their behalf. Ask God to bless them and come near to them in love and acceptance.

4. Think of three people who are hard to accept because of all the changes they need to make in their lives. Perhaps they are alcoholics, drug addicts, rebellious youth, homeless people, AIDS victims, someone who has committed adultery, or someone who has hurt you through criticism. Invite several of these people to your home for a special meal. Ask God to help you see them through His eyes. Accept them totally with no conditions or expectations of anything in return. Just love them, accept them, believe in them, and pray for them.

5. Go early to Sabbath School. Ask the Lord to lead you to those who need a word of affirmation and acceptance. Try to find at least ten people during the morning to whom you can show total, unconditional love and acceptance. Encourage them with a hug, a handshake of welcome, and words of appreciation and affirmation—regardless of how they are dressed or how they behave. Resolve not to let one word of criticism or denunciation escape your lips!

Explore in a group

1. Ask the group to share experiences when they were rejected, scolded, or criticized. How did it make them feel? Did it make them want to change?

2. Ask the group to share experiences when they were accepted unconditionally, loved, and affirmed without criticism or denunciation. How did it make them feel? Did it give them courage to want to be different?

3. Think of the person who was most responsible for helping you find the Lord or come into the church. What kind of person was he or she? How did he or she treat you? What was it about that person that made you want to become a Christian?

4. Discuss what your group could do to make your church a more accepting, believing, and praying church. What could

your members do to change the climate of the church?

5. Discuss the encounters Jesus had with fallen women. You may want to assign the following chapters of *The Desire of Ages* to study before the next meeting: "At Jacob's Well," "The Feast at Simon's House," "Lazarus, Come Forth," and "Among Snares." Look for Christ's method of facilitating change: Accept, Believe, Commit.

─────── 15 ───────

Bringing Blessing

The blessing of the Lord be upon you: we bless you in the name of the Lord (Psalm 129:8).

From the day Auntie had come to live in Ellen's home there had been unhappiness all around. Auntie nagged at the children and criticized Ellen. Ellen had tried to please the woman, but nothing she did was ever good enough. Her resentment building, Ellen at last decided to talk it over with her good friend Catherine Marshall.

"I don't know what to do about Auntie," Ellen sighed. "She nags the children constantly. They're getting fed up, and so am I. I've got to find some way to make her stop finding fault!"

"Have you prayed about it?" Catherine asked.

"Of course. I pray every day that God will change Auntie and make her easy to live with," Ellen answered. "It hasn't worked!"

"Why not forget about trying to change her?" Catherine suggested. "Why not just ask God to bless her, to make her happy."

"Hmmph!" Ellen answered. "She doesn't deserve it!" Then after a moment, she spoke thoughtfully, "But then neither do I. I guess none of us *deserves* God's blessing."

"Nothing we could ever do would be good enough to earn a scrap or a rag from His hands," Catherine agreed.

"Then let's ask God to bless Auntie right now," Ellen spoke with determination. "Pray with me, Catherine."

Ellen prayed something like this: "Bless Auntie in whatever

way she needs. Give her the gift of happiness."

Several days later, Ellen phoned Catherine. "This blessing business is dynamite! I've never seen Auntie so happy, and we're actually enjoying having her around!"[1]

Catherine Marshall calls praying for someone's happiness the prayer of joyous blessing. We can make a difference in people's lives through intercessory prayer.

Many people need our prayers of joyous blessing. However, without a plan for intercessory prayer, we could easily leave out some of those who need our prayers the most.

I've discovered that without some sort of outline for praying, my thoughts easily wander. One way is to have a prayer list. Another way is to use a memory device to help you cover all the areas of need. One such device is an acrostic based on the word *blessing*, each letter standing for one group of people for whom we want to pray: **B**urdens for family and friends, **L**eaders in the church, **E**nemies, **S**ick and suffering, **S**urvivors of disaster and abuse, **I**nterested people, **N**ew Christians, **G**overnment authorities.

Burdens for family and friends

Beginning with our nearest relatives, then working outward to include neighbors and friends, we can pray for their happiness. We can ask for the Holy Spirit to work on individual hearts, for angels to set a hedge about our loved ones, and for the specific blessings we know each one needs.

Ruth Bell Graham tells about a blessing she asked for when her five children were small. One night she went to bed discouraged because she had scolded all day.

"Dear God," she prayed, "please don't let the children remember my yelling at them so much!"

When daughter Gigi became a mother struggling with the frustrations of raising her own children, she found herself yelling a lot. She asked her mother, "Why is it that you never screamed at us when we were little?"

"You just don't remember," Ruth said with a chuckle. "I did it all the time." Then she told Gigi about her long-ago prayer.[2]

Leaders in the church

Conference leaders, pastors, and local church leaders need our prayers of joyous blessing.

One night I woke with a start, sure I had heard someone call my name. My husband continued to sleep soundly beside me, so I got up and toured the house to make sure nothing was wrong.

When I couldn't go back to sleep, I decided to pray for each of the pastors' wives in our conference, about sixty of them. One by one I took them to the Lord and asked Him to bless their homes, their marriages, and their ministry. Where I knew of specific needs, I presented those needs to the Lord too.

As soon as I completed the list, I went right back to sleep. I believe the Lord awoke me that winter night to pray for these pastoral partners in our conference. Someone needed the blessing that I could send her way on the wings of prayer.

Enemies

I once struggled with anger and bitterness toward a couple who had spread false reports about my husband. The more I thought about it, the deeper my anger grew.

Then the Lord began to work with me. "Dorothy, you need to forgive them. You need to love them, bless them, and pray for them." His voice was insistent.

"OK, Lord," I finally agreed halfheartedly. "I don't feel like it, but I choose to forgive them. Please bring happiness and blessing into their lives."

When angry thoughts came, I asked the Lord to bless the couple. Then I began to put my prayers into action. I greeted them warmly the next time we met instead of turning the other way. I found an occasion to give a little gift, and I wrote them a note when we were on vacation.

The Lord did His part too. The entire family really did seem to be happier than before. The best part was that the people were no longer my enemies, but my friends!

Sick and suffering

I am so thankful for scores of friends who prayed for me when

I had to have surgery for breast cancer. One morning I was particularly depressed. Overcome with a sense of my own mortality, I felt immobilized by the uncertainty of the future. After breakfast I went back to bed and lay there, thinking about a function we needed to attend that evening.

I didn't want to go. I didn't want to meet people, to talk about what I was going through. People would be watching to see how I'd handle this situation, and I didn't have the energy to put on a show of optimism and faith.

Already that morning, two friends had called, anxious to hear the news. But I refused to talk with them, letting Ron tell the bad news.

About ten o'clock, my friend Ruth Lennox called, insisting she talk to me. "I'm concerned about you," she said. "I dreamed about you last night, and I just had to call you and let you know how much I appreciate you. I have just read the chapter 'Eggs Expedition' in your book *Prayer Country*, and it was very meaningful to me. We love you, Dorothy, and we are praying for you."

I suddenly felt able to go on with life. I got up and worked at my computer for three hours before getting dressed for the function. Ruth blessed me joyously with her prayers!

Survivors of disasters and abuse

As I write this chapter, there is news of thousands left homeless in the worst flood to hit Italy since 1913. Many lost everything they owned; some lost their lives. Last week, there was a plane crash killing sixty-eight people. War still goes on in Bosnia. The refugee situation in Rwanda and Zaire is still horrendous. Here is plenty to pray about.

Also in today's news is the story of the funeral of two small boys in Union, South Carolina, who were allegedly murdered by their mother. While the boys' grandmother was interviewed, I cried with her as she shared her grief—and I prayed for her too. News that former President Ronald Reagan has Alzheimer's brought tears to my eyes as well. I prayed for him and his wife Nancy.

In most communities there are survivors of childhood abuse. These people need our prayers of joyous blessing. One of the most meaningful weekends I have ever spent was at a Take Heart Retreat conducted by Janis Vance. It was sponsored by our conference women's ministries department for women survivors of sexual abuse. Our group of prayer counselors arrived eight hours early to spend the day in prayer for the women who would come. Prayer counselors were on duty through every meeting and around the clock.

One woman, of another faith, said to me, "I didn't know what to expect this weekend. All I knew about Adventists was that they keep the Sabbath. I never knew you people prayed so much! It's a beautiful experience to be here, just to feel the Holy Spirit working in answer to prayer."

Many of the prayer counselors continue to pray for their assigned women every day. I have seen miracles happen as a result of those intercessory prayers for survivors of abuse.

Interested people

In every community people are searching for truth. They may be having Bible studies or watching a religious telecast. Perhaps they have attended evangelistic meetings, a stop-smoking seminar, or a vegetarian cooking class. These are all people for whom we can ask the special blessing of the Holy Spirit to guide them into all truth.

New Christians

A. G. Daniells—well-known minister, missionary, and seventh world president of the Seventh-day Adventist Church—was once a struggling new believer. Although he gave his heart to the Lord when he was ten years old and tried to be a good Christian, he often failed. Finally he just gave up, feeling it was no use. He stopped reading his Bible, praying, and giving his testimony.

One white-haired elder in his church noticed that something was wrong. After the benediction one Sabbath, he followed Arthur outside to where he hid among the shadows.

"I'm interested in you, Arthur," the old man said. "I've noticed that you've missed speaking in the service for three weeks now. What's the trouble?"

"There's no help for me," the boy mumbled. "I'll never make a Christian. I've tried and failed, so I've given up trying."

"You must not give up!" the elder declared. "I will pray for you this week every day. Now, will you try? Will you join me in prayer every day this week?"

Arthur agreed. The elder put his arm around Arthur's shoulders and drew him close. "Now, don't forget, I'll be praying for you every day!" he whispered. "You pray, too, and the Lord will help you. I know He will!"[3]

That was the turning point in Arthur Daniells's experience. One man's prayers had made a difference.

Government authorities

Many people were praying for attorney Karen Scott Hutton as she presented the plea for religious liberty in the case of Larry Renaud of Kelowna, British Columbia. He had been fired for not working on Sabbath.

There was a setback at the British Columbia Court of Appeal, but people kept praying, and Karen kept on working. Finally she was able to present Renaud's case before the seven justices of the Supreme Court of Canada. God answered prayer, and the judge ruled in favor of Renaud. This groundbreaking legal case means that employers now have a legal obligation to accommodate someone who requires an adjustment for Sabbath.[4]

A big God

Ifeoma Kwesi tells a wonderful story that happened when her five-year-old niece spent the night with her. After a bath, a bedtime story, a drink, and a trip to the bathroom, Ifeoma thought it was time for Christina to go to sleep so Ifeoma could get on with other duties.

Christina had other ideas. "I'm scared!" she said. "Can't you come to bed with me?"

"No need to be afraid," Ifeoma assured her. "Remember, we

prayed, and Jesus is going to take care of you."

"Humph! He can't even take care of Himself!"

"What do you mean?" Ifeoma was shocked.

"Well, He's just a little baby."

"No, He's not!"

"Yes, He is!" Christina insisted. "My teacher said that He was wrapped in swaddling clothes and lying in a manger."

Patiently Ifeoma explained that Jesus was all grown up, big and strong, and truly able to take care of her.

When she had finished, Christina breathed a happy sigh and snuggled down under the covers. Just before she closed her eyes, she said, "I'm glad He's big enough . . . aren't you?"[5]

Ah yes! God is big enough to handle all the people, problems, and perplexities we bring to Him in prayer. Our prayer list will never get beyond His power to cope. He is big enough to do more than we could ever ask or think.

Explore for yourself

1. Choose one of the letters of *BLESSING* to focus on this week. If it is "Survivors of Disaster and Abuse," use the daily news as a source of people and situations for intercessory prayer.

If it is "New Christians," take the time to make a list of all the new Christians you know. Ask God to show you some way to bless them this week. If it is "Enemies," take time to make a list of specific people you dislike or who have treated you badly. For one week, ask God to pour out His blessings upon them.

2. Make up your own acrostic for intercession. Trudy Vander Veen uses the word *powerfully* for her pattern of intercessory prayer: Political authorities, Oppressed and outcast people, Weak, wounded, and worried people, Emergencies on earth, Revival and readiness for Christ's return, Family, friends, and fellow Christians, Unsaved and uncommitted people, Leaders and laborers in the kingdom, Lonely and least, Yourself.[6]

3. Try a Spirit-directed list. This is the method used by Richard Foster. He writes, "After prayer for my immediate family, I wait quietly until individuals or situations sponta-

neously rise to my awareness. I then offer these to God, listening to see if any special discernment comes to guide the content of the prayer. Next, I speak forth what seems most appropriate in full confidence that God hears and answers. After spoken intercession I may remain for a while, inviting the Spirit to pray through me 'with sighs too deep for words.' I will stay with any given individual or situation until I feel released from the prayer concern. Throughout the time I may jot down brief notes in a small prayer journal as I sense the Spirit giving instruction. These notes are often extremely helpful, for over time a pattern sometimes emerges that holds the key to the person's need. This then informs the direction of future intercessions."[7]

Explore in a group

1. Work together as a group to make your own acrostic that will help you pray for the individuals and situations important to your group. Or divide into groups of three. Give each group a different word, and have them come up with their own acrostic.

2. Go through a Spirit-directed time of intercession in your group. Wait prayerfully in silence until someone is impressed about a need. Then pray for that individual or situation. Two or three others join in, agreeing in prayer about that need. Wait quietly until someone else is moved to pray for a specific person.

3. Divide into eight smaller groups. Give each group one letter of the word *blessing*. They are to pray for the group of people that comes under that letter, as suggested in this chapter. The group should first brainstorm, making a list of all who need their prayers under that heading. Then they can have a time of intercession, praying through their list.

—————16—————

Making a Difference

Pray ye therefore the Lord of the harvest, that he would send forth labourers into his harvest (Luke 10:2).

Consider the challenge of Adventist Global Mission!

• The ratio of non-Christians to Christians is 2 to 1. Out of a world population of over 5 billion, approximately 3.5 billion have been unreached with the gospel of Jesus Christ.

• If every Christian in the world were to win his or her neighbor to Christ, there would still be over 2.5 billion non-Christians unreached. Someone must cross cultural-linguistic barriers to share the message of God's love with them.

• Giving for the support of the regular mission program of the church is declining, making it necessary to cut appropriations to the very areas of the world that need the most help.

• While Adventists have a presence in most of the world's countries, we are a long way from having "memorials for Him in every city and village."[1]

• Every second, three babies are born. That's more than a quarter million babies a day, more than 100 million babies a year. That is equivalent of one new China in ten years! China already has as many people as Europe, North America, and South America combined.

At this rate, the world population in 2030 would exceed 10 billion, nearly double today's population.[2]

The task seems overwhelming! The goal of taking the message to every "nation, kindred, tongue, and people" appears impossible to achieve! The barriers of language, culture, religion, and the apathy of God's people seem too difficult to surmount. How can so few do so much? Could intercessory prayer be the answer?

The one-hundred-year prayer meeting

A marvelous prayer vigil began in the exiled Moravian community of Herrnhut in Saxony in 1727. Led by Count Zinzendorf, a group of twenty-four men and twenty-four women covenanted to spend one hour each day in scheduled prayer for a lost world. Soon others joined them in the hourly prayer.

Just as the sacred fire on the altar of the tabernacle was never permitted to go out, the prayers of that community continued around the clock without ceasing for one hundred years!

As a result, within six months, twenty-six of the group volunteered for world missions. By 1792, sixty-five years after the beginning of the prayer vigil, that small community had sent out three hundred missionaries. It was Moravian missionaries from this community who witnessed to John Wesley. That led to the Great Awakening in England and America during the eighteenth century.[3]

The haystack prayer meeting

Another example of the power of prayer in world missions is what happened during a thunderstorm on the campus of Williams College, Williamstown, Massachusetts, in 1806.

Five young men were headed for some willows near the college to have a prayer meeting when rain began to fall. The nearest shelter was a haystack. The rain kept up for some time, and the students turned their discussion to foreign missions.

"I think it's time we in America sent missionaries to foreign fields," declared Samuel Mills, the leader. "While we wait, millions are going into Christless graves."

When others objected, saying that they were only students

and not yet ready to go as missionaries, Samuel replied, "What you say is true, but we can do all we can to stimulate interest in missions in our school. We can talk to experienced pastors and convince them of our idea. We can do it if we will!"

The five agreed and began to pray for a revival of the missionary spirit. As a result, the first American missionary society was formed. Adoniram Judson and five other missionaries were sent to India. What followed was the great century of world missions.

A marble globe sitting atop a large granite shaft on the campus of Williams College commemorates that event. On it are chiseled the words "The Birthplace of Foreign Missions, 1806" and "The field is the world."[4]

The field is still the world. The harvest is ripe, but the reapers are few. Thousands are needed who will pray the Lord of harvest to send forth reapers.

It all begins with prayer

"Every step in the progress of missions is directly traceable to prayer," writes A. T. Pierson. "It has been the preparation for every new triumph and the secret of all success."[5]

The journals of David Brainerd, missionary to the native people of North America, are full of his agonizing intercession on behalf of these people. About the results of those prayers, he recorded:

God's manner of working upon them seemed so entirely supernatural and above means, that I could scarcely believe He used me as an instrument. I seemed to do nothing, and indeed to have nothing to do but to 'stand still and see the salvation of God.' God appeared to work entirely alone, and I saw no room to attribute any part of this work to any created man.[6]

Clifford Howell observed, "It is the humble, praying man that accomplishes for God. Pentecost is separated from us not so much by years as by unbelief."[7]

While working as a cobbler, William Carey read Captain Cook's

Voyages Around the World and became concerned about those who had never heard the name of Jesus. He began immediately to make their salvation a matter of earnest intercession. He prayed for several years that the Lord would open people's eyes to the needs of a lost world. He tried to share his burden, but fellow ministers wouldn't listen. He continued to pray until another opportunity came to express his concern.

Carey was asked to speak at a meeting of ministers. He spoke on Isaiah 54:2, 3: "Enlarge the place of thy tent." During his message, he made a statement that became the motto for missions during the next century: "Expect great things from God: attempt great things for God."

As a result of Carey's prayers, the Lord moved upon the hearts of those present, and a missionary society was formed. William Carey was sent to India, where he spent forty years and translated the Bible into forty different languages.[8]

Hudson Taylor established the China Inland Mission on prayer alone. Every one of the workers who joined him in China was an answer to prayer. He resolved to never ask for money of anyone but God. When he gave up leadership of the mission, there were 849 missionaries, 1,282 national workers, 837 mission stations, 188 schools, and 44 hospitals and dispensaries—all the result of intercessory prayer.[9]

Columba, Livingstone, and Whitefield died while praying for others. John Knox pleaded with God, "Give me Scotland or I die." Behind every great missionary effort has been prayer.[10]

"We can reach our world, if we will," declares Wesley L. Duewel in his book *Touch the World Through Prayer.* He continues:

> The greatest lack today is not people or funds. The greatest need is prayer. Without increasing the number of Christian workers or their financial support, we could see multiplied results if we would only multiply prayer.[11]

Prayer possibilities

What might happen if one person in each Adventist church would begin to pray in earnest for Global Mission? With more than 35,000 churches scattered throughout the twenty-four time zones, more than 1,500 prayers per hour would be ascending on behalf of world missions. Think of the power that could have!

What should we pray for? We can pray for people, resources, awareness, and the yielding of barriers. We can pray for the Holy Spirit to open and convict hearts.

People. Pray for people to cross cultural barriers to reap the harvest. We need missionaries from every place, not just North America, Europe, and Australia, to go to an unreached people group with God's message. We need missionaries going from everywhere to everywhere.

Resources. Our existing work must be supported and strengthened. Workers need to be trained. The means for new ventures must be funded. If every church member were to give a minimum of 2 percent of his or her income for world missions, abundant funds would be available to do what must be done. Mission offerings would skyrocket, and marvelous things could be done.

Awareness. In some places Adventists seem to have lost the vision of a finished work. We need to pray for a renewal of awareness in every church member to the tremendous needs and opportunities of a world lost without Christ. We need to pray for our eyes to be opened that we may view the world as Christ does.

Yielding. We can pray for the yielding of barriers in specific areas of the world. We can pray for the yielding of hearts to the Holy Spirit as missionaries cross cultural boundaries to share Christ.[12]

Holy Spirit. We can pray for an outpouring of the Holy Spirit, for we know that it "brings all other blessings in its train."[13]

I believe that through the power of the Holy Spirit and prayer, the best days of Global Mission are just ahead!

Explore for yourself

1. Make a Global Mission prayer list. Gordon MacDonald includes missions in his intercessory prayer time. In order to

systematically pray around the world, he has divided the continents in such a way that he can pray each day for one of them:

Sunday, South America; Monday, Central America; Tuesday, North America; Wednesday, Europe; Thursday, Africa; Friday, Asia; and Saturday, the Pacific nations. In each area he includes intercession for the national church, for missionaries with whom he is acquainted, and for the suffering that people face in that area.[14]

2. Try Dick Eastman's fifteen-minute plan. He notes that God gives us ninety-six fifteen-minute time periods every day. He suggests we set aside one or two of these for intercessory prayer for family, friends, and the world. His instructions are:[15]

First Five Minutes: Use it for praise, adoration, and worship. Take time to love God because He is God. Remember that we enter the gates of heaven by thanksgiving and praise.

Second Five Minutes: Pray for needs close to you: family, local-area concerns, your church, your pastor, your community, and your friends.

Third Five Minutes: Pray for specific countries of the world. Since there are 210 separate geographical areas, it would take most of the time to just name the countries. He suggests dividing the 210 countries into groups of 30 countries, praying for one set each day. Thus in one week you could cover the whole world. Ask the Lord to open doors, provide laborers, and supply funds to meet the needs of the work.

3. Pray through your Sabbath School quarterly. Pray for each country shown on the map on back of the quarterly, concentrating on the needs of that division. Read the brief mission stories that are interspersed between lessons. Pray for the persons and institutions mentioned.

Explore in a group

1. Adopt a country or a people group. Write to Global Mission, 12501 Old Columbia Pike, Silver Spring, Maryland 20904. Ask for information about the unreached areas of the globe. Pick one area or people group as your target. Research that area to learn

all you can about it. Interview people from that area, and find out what is being done to reach those people. Then pray daily for that area. Thank God as you see things begin to happen.

2. Discuss the message of the three angels in Revelation 14. What is our task as Adventists? Is it to reach out to those who have never heard the gospel, or is it simply to take the three angels' messages to those who are already Christians? Is our message for all people of the world, or only for non-Christians?

3. Brainstorm about what your group could do to obey the mission mandate for every Christian to go into all the world and preach the gospel to every creature. Have a time of prayer, asking God to show you what you could do to get more involved.

4. Plan a concentrated prayer effort for Global Mission. It might be a prayer chain, an all-night prayer meeting, or a plan where members pledge to pray at a certain time each day.

References

Introduction: The Treasure

1. Ellen G. White, *Sons and Daughters of God,* 125.
2. Dorothy Eaton Watts, *This Is the Day* (Hagerstown, Md.: Review and Herald Publishing Assn., 1982), 144.

Chapter 1: Pursuing God

1. Ellen G. White, *Steps to Christ,* 94.
2. Dorothy Eaton Watts, *Prayer Country* (Nampa, Idaho: Pacific Press Publishing Assn., 1993), 7-11.
3. Gordon MacDonald, *Ordering Your Private World* (Nashville, Tenn: Thomas Nelson Publishers, 1985).
4. *Prayer Country,* 15-20.

Chapter 2: Searching for Reality

1. Jacquelyn Wonder and Priscilla Donovan, *Whole-Brain Thinking* (New York: Ballantine Books, 1984).
2. Arlene Taylor, *Gender Graphics: Insights Into the Human Brain* (Napa, Calif.: Realizations, 1990).
3. *Seventh-day Adventist Hymnal*, no. 281.
4. Kenneth W. Osbeck, *101 Hymn Stories* (Grand Rapids, Mich.: Kregel Publications, 1982), 102.
5. Charles H. Spurgeon, *Twelve Sermons on Prayer* (Grand Rapids, Mich.: Baker Book House, 1990), 25, 21.
6. *Steps to Christ,* 99, 100.

Chapter 3: Sensing Reality

1. Ellen G. White, *Early Writings,* 11, 12, 79, 80.
2. Marlene LeFever, "Pictures and Words and Hummingbird Wings," *Virtue,* September/October 1989, 16.
3. Monte Sahlin, "Three Worship Models," *ABBA,* May/June 1991, 6.
4. Walter B. Barbe and Michael N. Milone, Jr., "What We Know About Modality Strengths," *Educational Leadership,* February 1981, 378-380.
5. *Gender Graphics,* 23, 24.
6. Elizabeth R. Skoglund, *Wounded Heroes* (Grand Rapids, Mich.: Baker Book House, 1992), 50, 51.

Chapter 4: Discovering Praise

1. Rose Otis, ed., *Among Friends* (Hagerstown, Md.: Review and Herald, 1992), 382, 383.
2. *Steps to Christ,* 104.
3. Catherine Marshall, *Light in My Darkest Night* (New York: Avon Books, 1989), 198-221.
4. Ellen G. White, *Christ's Object Lessons,* 129.
5. *101 Hymn Stories,* 24.

Chapter 5: Seeking Solitude

1. Anne Morrow Lindbergh, *Gift From the Sea* (New York: Random House, Inc., 1983), 45, 48-53.
2. Richard J. Foster, *Celebration of Disicipline* (San Francisco: Harper and Row, 1988), 96-109.
3. Debra Anne Bell, "Six Steps to Consistent Prayer," *Virtue,* May/June 1990, 14.
4. Ibid., 15.
5. Ellen G. White, *The Desire of Ages,* 363.
6. Ellen G. White, *The Ministry of Healing,* 509.
7. Richard J. Foster, *Study Guide for Celebration of Discipline* (San Francisco: Harper and Row, 1983), 45.
8. Ibid.

Chapter 6: Finding Friendship

1. *101 Hymn Stories,* 276.
2. Matilda Erickson Andross, *Alone With God* (Nampa, Idaho: Pacific Press, 1929), 37.
3. *Steps to Christ,* 99, 100.

4. Ibid., 93.
5. Ibid., 100.
6. Ibid.
7. Jim Conway, *Making Real Friends in a Phony World* (Grand Rapids, Mich.: Zondervan Publishing, 1989), 69-85.
8. *Steps to Christ,* 93.
9. *Alone With God*, 35.

Chapter 7: Getting Guidance

1. *This Is the Day,* 116.
2. Dorothy Eaton Watts, "God's Plan," *Adventist Review,* 13 October 1983, 26, 27.
3. Irene Burk Harrell, comp., *God Ventures: True Accounts of God in the Lives of Men* (Plainfield, N.J.: Logos International, 1970), 34-40.
4. Gordon MacDonald, *Ordering Your Private World*, expanded edition (Nashville, Tenn.: Thomas Nelson, 1985), 130.
5. Judith C. Lechman, *The Spirituality of Gentleness: Growing Toward Christian Wholeness* (San Francisco: Harper and Row, 1987), 73, 74.
6. Ellen G. White, *Testimonies for the Church,* 4:542.
7. Charles Stanley, *How to Listen to God* (Nashville, Tenn.: Thomas Nelson, 1985), 49-63.
8. William K. Reichard, "I Heard the Voice of an Angel," *NPUC Gleaner,* 2 February 1987, 6.

Chapter 8: Finding Grace

1. Jacob Gartenhaus, *Famous Hebrew Christians* (Chattanooga, Tenn.: International Board of Jewish Missions, Inc., 1979), 95-97.
2. H. M. S. Richards, *The Promises of God* (Hagerstown, Md.: Review and Herald, 1956), 264.
3. Richard J. Foster, *Prayer: Finding the Heart's True Home* (San Francisco: HarperCollins, 1992), 4.
4. Ellen G. White, *Testimonies for the Church,* 6:364.
5. *Prayer,* 8.
6. Wayne Hooper and Edward White, *Companion to the Seventh-day Adventist Hymnal* (Hagerstown, Md.: Review and Herald, 1988).

Chapter 9: Visioning Victory

1. Julie A. Talerico, "Elizabeth Mittelstaedt: Influencing a Nation," *Today's Christian Woman,* January/February 1992, 24-27, 68.
2. *The Desire of Ages,* 120, 121.
3. Ellen G. White, *The Great Controversy,* 530.

4. Ellen G. White, *The Acts of the Apostles,* 564.
5. Ellen G. White, *Testimonies for the Church,* 1:346.
6. Quoted in Joe Engelkemeir, *Whatever It Takes Praying* (Fallbrook, Calif.: Hart Research Center, 1993), 93.
7. *The Desire of Ages,* 240.
8. *The Great Controversy,* 559.
9. Ibid., 560.

Chapter 10: Obtaining Healing

1. *Wounded Heroes,* 149.
2. *Christ's Object Lessons,* 171, 172.
3. Joyce Landorf, *The High Cost of Growing* (Toronto: Bantam Books, 1978), 31-59.
4. Ibid., 40.
5. Dale Hanson Bourke, "Joni at 40," *Today's Christian Woman,* January/February 1990, 23-25, 68.
6. *The Ministry of Healing,* 241.

Chapter 11: Gathering Joy

1. *The World Book Encyclopedia,* 6:47.
2. *Wounded Heroes,* 160.
3. Frank Houghton, *Amy Carmichael of Dohnavur* (Fort Washington, Penn.: Christian Literature Crusade, 1953, 1979), 289-295.
4. Gail MacDonald, *Keep Climbing* (Wheaton, Ill.: Tyndale House Publishers, Inc., 1989), 168, 169.
5. Etty Hillesum, *An Interrupted Life* (New York: Washington Square Press, 1981), 207, quoted in *Keep Climbing,* 224.
6. *Keep Climbing,* 225.
7. *Steps to Christ,* 117.
8. Ibid.
9. Lucinda Secrest McDowell, "Escape the Trap of Loneliness," *Virtue,* July/August 1989, 37-40.

Chapter 12: Seeking Peace

1. *The Church Hymnal,* no. 311.
2. *101 Hymn Stories,* 206, 207.
3. Elisabeth Elliot, *Discipline: The Glad Surrender* (Tarrytown, N.J.: Fleming H. Revell, Co., 1982), 155.
4. Ibid., 14.
5. Ellen G. White, *Life Sketches,* 21.
6. Ibid., 23, 24.

7. *The Ministry of Healing*, 417.

8. Ellen G. White, *Education*, 305.

Chapter 13: Discovering Power

1. Norman Vincent Peale, ed., *Treasury of Joy and Enthusiasm* (Old Tappan, N.J.: Fleming H. Revell), 184-187.

2. Dick Eastman, *No Easy Road* (Grand Rapids, Mich.: Baker Book House, 1971), 58.

3. *Prayer,* 191.

4. E. M. Bounds, *Power Through Prayer* (Springdale, Penn.: Whitaker House, 1982), 31.

5. Wesley L. Duewel, *Touch the World Through Prayer* (Grand Rapids, Mich.: Francis Asbury Press of Zondervan Publishing House, 1986), 39-44.

6. Quoted in Dick Eastman, *The Hour That Changes the World* (Grand Rapids, Mich.: Baker Book House, 1978), 76.

7. *Prayer,* 191.

8. Morris Venden, *The Answer Is Prayer* (Nampa, Idaho: Pacific Press Publishing Assn., 1988), 53-55.

9. Ibid., 55, 56.

10. Quoted in *The Hour That Changes the World*, 13.

11. *No Easy Road,* 66.

12. *Alone With God,* 74.

13. Ibid., 77.

14. *This Is the Day,* 325.

15. John Calvin, *Sermons on the Epistle to the Ephesians* (Edinburgh: Banner of Truth Trust, 1975), 683.

16. Nancy Van Pelt, *Prayer Notebook* (Hagerstown, Md.: Review and Herald, 1993).

17. *Prayer Country,* 23-29.

18. Ibid., 23-28.

Chapter 14: Facilitating Change

1. J. Grant Swank, Jr., "The Best Daddy," *Decision*, June 1991, 42.

2. *The Desire of Ages,* 272.

3. Ibid., 274.

4. Ibid., 189.

5. *Education,* 114.

6. *The Desire of Ages,* 183-195.

7. Ibid., 91.

8. Ibid., 568.

9. Ibid., 291, 292.

10. Ibid., 568.

11. Ibid., 190.

12. Randy Miller, "The Cold Fist of Love," *World Vision,* September/October 1990, 23.

Chapter 15: Bringing Blessing

1. Catherine Marshall, *Adventures in Prayer* (Old Tappan, N.J.: Chosen Books, Fleming H. Revell Co., 1975), 73-75.

2. Julie Nixon Eisenhower, *Special People* (New York: Simon and Schuster, 1977), 76.

3. May Cole Kuhn, *Leader of Men: The Life of Arthur G. Daniells* (Hagerstown, Md.: Review and Herald, 1946), 22-25.

4. "Karen Scott Hutton: Outstanding Achievement," *The Adventist Woman,* August/September 1994, 1, 2.

5. Rose Otis, ed. *The Listening Heart* (Hagerstown, Md.: Review and Herald, 1993), 76, 77.

6. Trudy Vander Veen, "Pray Powerfully," *Discipleship Journal,* no. 29, 1985, 33-35.

7. *Prayer,* 200.

Chapter 16: Making a Difference

1. Dorothy Eaton Watts, "Prayer and World Missions: So Much to Do," *Sabbath School Worker*, April-June 1989, 12, 13.

2. *The Canadian Global Almanac, 1993* (Toronto: Macmillan Canada, 1992), 254, 255.

3. Leslie K. Tarr, "A Prayer Meeting That Lasted 100 Years," *Christian History*, vol. 1, no. l.

4. Clifford G. Howell, *The Advance Guard of Missions* (Nampa, Idaho: Pacific Press Publishing Assn., 1912), 133-145.

5. *The Hour That Changes the World,* 78.

6. *The Advance Guard of Missions,* 31-44.

7. Ibid., 84-100.

8. Ibid., 299-323.

9. Ibid., 319.

10. *Alone With God*, 31.

11. *Touch the World Through Prayer, 13*.

12. Dorothy Eaton Watts, *Sabbath School Worker,* April-June 1989, 13.

13. *The Desire of Ages,* 672.

14. *Ordering Your Private World*, 156.

15. *No Easy Road,* 124, 125.